Munchie Madness

Vegetarian Meals for Teens

Recipes by

Dorothy Bates, Bobbie Hinman, Robert Oser

Nutritional Information by

Suzanne Havala, MS, RD, FADA

Book Publishing Company
Summertown, Tennessee

Cover design: Estelle Carrol
Interior design: Gwynelle Dismukes
Drawings and cover concept: Lenny Cramer

Printed in the United States by
Book Publishing Company
P.O. Box 99
Summertown, TN 38483
1-888-260-8458
www.bookpubco.com

ISBN 1-57067-115-X

07 06 05 04 03 02 01   9 8 7 6 5 4 3 2 1

Bates, Dorothy R., 1921-
  Munchie madness : vegetarian meals for teens / Dorothy Bates, Bobbie Hinman, Robert Oser ; introduction, Suzanne Havala.
       p. cm.
Includes index.
  ISBN 1-57067-115-X (alk. paper)
  1. Vegetarian cookery--Juvenile literature. [1. Vegetarian cookery. 2. Vegetarianism. 3. Nutrition.] I. Hinman, Bobbie. II. Oser, Robert, 1948- III. Title.
  TX837 .B338 2001
  641.5′636--dc21   2001001337

Calculations for the nutritional analyses in this book are based on the average number of servings listed with the recipes and the average amount of an ingredient if a range is called for. Calculations are rounded up to the nearest gram. If two options for an ingredient are listed, the first one is used. Not included are optional ingredients or serving suggestions.

CONTENTS

A word to parents

If you're a parent of teenagers, you might swear your children don't listen to a word you say, but in actuality they do. Our young people have listened carefully to our concerns about the state of the environment and the need to care for our fellow creatures; many of them have responded by becoming vegetarians.

If you are not a vegetarian yourself, this may seem like cause for concern, but it doesn't need to be. We have compiled this cookbook (using recipes from some of the country's most acclaimed vegetarian cookbook authors) to provide easy and nutritious meal ideas that you, your teen, and your entire family will enjoy. Registered dietitian and author Suzanne Havala also presents a section on vegetarian nutrition that is up to date and easy to understand, so you can help your teen vegetarian make the best food choices.

Many of us here at Book Publishing Company have raised healthy vegetarian youngsters from birth through their teenage years. We are proud of their choice to continue a vegetarian lifestyle, knowing it will lead to a legacy of good health for them and a safer environment for the planet.

Cynthia Holzapfel
Senior Editor
Book Publishing Company

Notes from a Vegetarian Teen

For most teens the reason for going vegetarian differs from what motivates most adults. We choose vegetarianism because of the cruelty to animals, what the hormones from meat do to our bodies at such a vulnerable age, and the large impact that the meat industry has on the environment. I was raised vegetarian and I have learned about this all my life—and I'm still learning. I am so grateful to my parents for raising me in a vegetarian lifestyle.

1 Cruelty to animals

Unfortunately, death is probably one of the least cruel acts that humans inflict on industry animals. Chickens and most other poultry are packed together in cages so tightly that they can barely move a wing. Chickens were meant to live outside and scratch at the ground for food. They also have a natural instinct to develop a society with a matriarchal hen. In these cages (which are stacked in dark barns with little air movement) the chickens' claws grow so long that they hook around the cage to the point that the birds can no longer move or reach their food. Since the hens are still trying to form their society and there are so many chickens in one cage, the struggle for dominance is endless. The hens will badly hurt one another and even kill each other, hence the term "pecking order." To prevent the loss of chickens from starvation and killing each other, farmers will cut off part of their toes, just after the start of the claw. Also, farmers cut the ends of the chickens' beaks off, a process known as debeaking.

Baby male cows (calves) are taken away at birth and fed a diet that specifically deprives them of essential nutrients so they will make a more tender veal. They will also look for any thing to suck on, as they are denied the right to suckle. Once on a trip with my family, we passed a fenced-in area containing what looked like dog igloos. I thought at first it was a pound, but really it was a veal farm. These calves were chained to their own plastic igloos and had just enough chain to get in and out of their houses. They did not have any grass to graze on, just dry hay and feed.

When a cow is slaughtered, it's first stunned; this is done in a few different ways. Some cows are shot in the head with a large bolt that may or may not render them unconscious, some are electrocuted, some are hit in the head with a blunt object, and I'm sure there are more methods I haven't heard of. Then the cows are strung up by their back legs, dangling along an assembly line waiting for their turn. Their throats are cut and then they are disemboweled. Each year 150,000 of these cows are pregnant, many of them are near full term. When the pregnant cow is disemboweled, the womb falls onto the concrete floor where the baby thrashes about and drowns in its own fluids.

I could go on about the extent of cruelty toward all industry animals; pigs, cows, and chickens are probably the largest groups. Disease spreads quickly among them, as they have to walk around in their own feces and are barely able to move.

② Hormones and chemicals

Industry animals are fed a variety of additives to keep them from getting sick and to help them grow more quickly. Hens are fed hormones so they will produce more eggs, and virtually all industry animals are given hormones, similar to estrogen and testosterone, to make them fatter. Since the use of these additives in livestock began, doctors have seen a steady lowering of the age at which girls start puberty. These hormones may affect adults also, but they are more likely to harm us teenage girls with longer lasting effects. And at this age we already have so many hormones running slightly wild in our bodies, do we really need more? Scientists are studying the many possible affects of these hormones, including the increase in child molestation, identity confusion, and other behavior disorders due to an imbalance in sex hormones. There have been cases of boys developing breasts and girls starting menstruation as early as five years old.

Another additive used in the animal industry that affects humans is antibiotics. Because of their poor living conditions, the animals become sick easily, so they are fed antibiotics and other disease-preventing chemicals in large quantities. These additives stay in the meat, milk, and eggs and are transferred to you when you eat them. They may weaken your immune system, and the younger you are, the less time your immune system has had to develop naturally. Antibiotics can be in infant formulas or in the breast milk of a mother who eats meat and dairy products.

3 Wasting the world's resources

One thing that's important to realize is the foods that animals eat are similar to foods eaten by humans. Instead of feeding livestock so we can consume them, we can consume the foods they do instead. The mass production of animal feed is hard on the environment. Sixteen pounds of soybeans when fed to a cow results in one pound of beef. You can take the same 16 pounds of soybeans and end up with 48 to 64 pounds of tofu. The numbers are similar when comparing grain fed to animals with that needed to make bread.

Another environmental impact to consider is the consumption of water. A cow can drink eight to nine gallons of water a day, not to mention the water used to grow the food it eats and the amount of cow dung washed into local water systems. A study in California found that it takes nearly 2,500 gallons of water to produce 1 pound of beef, which is almost 4 times more than that needed to produce the same amount of chicken, and incredibly over 10 times more than that needed to produce 1 pound of tofu. Industry animal manure is now the leading cause of water pollution. It causes algae bloom that may choke out other natural aquatic life. For every pound of meat, including chicken, we lose about five pounds of top soil. Much more packaging has to be used for meat. and all that packaging ends up in landfills.

Producing meat also uses up gasoline. Gasoline is a large contributor to pollution itself and is also a precious resource in today's world. In the animal industry, gasoline fuels the farm equipment used to grow corn, sorghum, and soybeans for the animals to eat. Pigs are just about the biggest eaters and pound for pound use up more energy than any other industry animal. It takes almost half a gallon of gasoline to make one pound of pork, a quarter gallon to produce one pound of beef, and about a fifth of a gallon to produce one pound of poultry.

Make a difference—it's easy!

As you can see, there are many good reasons to become vegetarian. Becoming a vegetarian doesn't mean you have to change much about your life. Even vegetarian food isn't really that different. Just about anything you can make with meat you can make just as good with tofu or other meat substitute—or you can just leave the meat out, like with cheese pizza, or use your favorite nonmeat toppings. This book was designed to help ease the transition from meat-eater to non-meat-eater. It takes some of the most common recipes (and some more exotic), and shows you easy ways to make them deliciously vegetarian. There are also snack items and other quick foods that will help ensure you get all the nutrition you need. There isn't any nutrient in meat that you can't get plenty of from another source. Think of how much good you can do yourself and the environment by not eating just one hamburger!

Laura Holzapfel
Summertown, Tenn.

Vegetarian Nutrition: A Primer for Teens

Are you considering a switch to a vegetarian diet? Have you already pushed the meat off your plate? If so, then you're in good company. According to a 2000 Vegetarian Resource Group-sponsored National Zogby Poll, about 2 percent of people ages 13 to 17 years never eat meat, fish, or poultry. Based on U.S. Census Bureau information, that number translates into nearly a half million teen vegetarians.

The reasons for going vegetarian are as varied as teens themselves. You might be motivated by efforts to save the environment from damage caused by intensive animal agriculture practices, or you might do it out of compassion for animals and to take a stand for nonviolence. The health advantages of a meat-free diet are another compelling reason to go vegetarian. Vegetarians have an easier time controlling their weight, and they have lower rates of coronary artery disease, some types of cancer, high blood pressure, diabetes, and other ills. If you're looking for a reason to go vegetarian, you don't have to look far.

If you're already a vegetarian, the chances are good that you're the only one in your family. That means that your mom and dad are likely to have little experience or knowledge about vegetarian diets. Even your teacher, other relatives, friends, and your doctor or other health care provider are unlikely to have personal experience with a vegetarian lifestyle. For the people that care about you, your vegetarianism can generate some tension over such issues as nutrition and fitting in socially with the rest of your family and friends.

These subjects can even be issues in homes where vegetarianism is the norm. As a teen, you are still going through a period of rapid growth and development. The people who love you will want to know that you are getting what you need to be healthy. The good news is a vegetarian diet can supply all the nutrients you need to keep you healthy throughout your life. The hitch is you have to follow some common sense guidelines to eating well. Soft drinks and French fries are vegetarian, but a junk food diet is a junk food diet—vegetarian or not. For optimal health, people of all ages need diets that are rich in nutrient-packed fruits, vegetables, whole grains, and legumes. That's especially important in the growing years. Let's look at what it takes to eat a healthful vegetarian diet and how to survive in a meat-eating, fast-food culture.

GOING VEGETARIAN: A HEALTHY CHOICE FOR TEENS

It's not only safe to be a vegetarian, it's better for your health if you are one. In its position paper on vegetarian diets, the American Dietetic Association states:

> It is the position of The American Dietetic Association (ADA) that appropriately planned vegetarian diets are healthful, are nutritionally adequate, and provide health benefits in the prevention and treatment of certain diseases.

The ADA also says vegetarian diets are fine both for children and teens:

> Well-planned vegan and lacto-ovo-vegetarian diets are appropriate for all stages of the life cycle, including during pregnancy and lactation. Appropriately planned vegan and lacto-ovo-vegetarian diets satisfy nutrient needs of infants, children, and adolescents and promote normal growth.

> Vegetarian Diets Position of ADA.
> Journal of the American Dietetic Association, 1997

Despite this official endorsement, you might get some resistance from health care providers when you express an interest in going vegetarian. Instead of encouraging and supporting the move, some health professionals might try to talk you out of it, and react with an emotional response that is not supported by science. For those who have not had personal experience with a vegetarian lifestyle, acceptance and understanding can be difficult. Moreover, some professionals are simply not up to date on the nutrition issues.

So it's a good idea to get knowledgeable *yourself* about vegetarian nutrition. Armed with the facts, you'll be in a good position to dispel the concerns of the people who care about you. You'll also help ensure your success at crafting and maintaining a healthful vegetarian eating style.

The ABCs of Vegetarian Nutrition

Vegetarian teens have the same nutritional requirements as non-vegetarian teens. When it comes to eating well, a few key nutrients deserve special attention.

Protein Power ➤ There's rarely a need for vegetarians to worry about getting enough protein in their diets. The fact is, most nonvegetarians eat far too much protein. Vegetarians tend to eat less protein; they get enough, but they don't get too much.

In fact, some of the health benefits that vegetarians enjoy are a direct result of eating less protein. Higher consumption of animal protein is associated with higher rates of coronary artery disease, kidney disease, and some forms of cancer. Higher protein intakes also cause our bones to lose calcium. In nonvegetarians, this translates into higher rates of osteoporosis—a disease characterized by bones that are brittle and easily broken. Many health care providers then recommend extra high amounts of calcium to compensate for losses caused by eating an excessive amount of protein.

How Much is Enough?

If you are interested in knowing how much protein your body needs in a day, here is the rule of thumb that nutritionists use to determine protein needs:

0.8 grams of protein per kilogram of body weight. (One kilogram is equal to 2.2 pounds.)

So, if you weigh 125 pounds, that's equal to 57 kilograms (125 pounds divided by 2.2 pounds per kilogram). If you multiply 57 kilograms times 0.8 grams of protein per kilogram, that's equal to about 46 grams of protein.

Forty-six grams of protein isn't much, and that figure includes a generous margin of error.

How Easy is it to Get 46 Grams of Protein a Day?

Following are some examples of the protein content of various foods:

Food	Protein (grams)
8 ounces of plain soymilk	10
One veggie burger with bun (depending on the recipe)	10-30
4 ounces of tempeh	20
1 cup vegetarian chili	24
1 cup black bean soup	16
Bean burrito	8
½ cup vegetarian baked beans	6
Whole bagel	6
Peanut butter sandwich	20
1 cup of most vegetables	4
1 cup of cooked oatmeal	6
1 cup of cooked plain pasta	14

There are two simple keys to getting enough protein on a vegetarian diet. They are:

✓ Get enough calories to meet your energy needs.

✓ Eat a reasonable variety of foods, including fruits, vegetables, grains, and legumes, nuts, and seeds.

That's it. Lack of calories (or food) goes hand in hand with protein deficiency. If you are eating (a) enough food to maintain a normal, healthy weight, and (b) a reasonable variety of foods, then you are extremely unlikely to become protein deficient.

THE CALCIUM CONNECTION ➤ As a teen, your body is busy building bones that are dense with calcium. From childhood through about the age of 35, your body is working towards achieving peak bone mass, the most calcium and bone mass that you will ever have in your life and the strongest that your bones are ever likely to be. After that, you will slowly lose calcium from your bones as you age. The more calcium you can store up while you are young, the more likely you are to stave off the debilitating effects of osteoporosis, a disease of brittle, easily broken bones that is common in many older adults.

SOME VEGETARIAN FOODS ESPECIALLY RICH IN PROTEIN:

Soymilk and fruit smoothies
Tofu salad
Tempeh sloppy Joes
Bean burritos
Lentil soup
Vegetable lasagne
Veggie burgers and dogs
Vegetarian chili
Hummus with pita bread
Bean soup
Peanut butter on celery or
   apple slices
Vegetarian pizza
Stir-fried vegetables and
   tofu over rice
Black beans and rice

Most of us associate eating foods with lots of calcium with strong bones, but it's actually not as simple as that. What's more important to bone health than the amount of calcium you get in your diet is the amount of calcium that your body absorbs and retains. The two dietary factors that most affect your body's ability to hang onto calcium are how much protein and sodium you eat. In particular, animal protein has a great effect on your body's ability to retain calcium.

When you eat meat and other forms of animal protein, your blood becomes more acidic. Your body neutralizes this acid by buffering it with calcium pulled from your bones. Eventually the calcium works its way to your kidneys where it is filtered out and lost in your urine. Scientists estimate that the ideal dietary ratio is about 16 milligrams of calcium to 1 gram of protein. In other words, if you are a vegetarian getting about 45 grams of protein in your daily diet, you should get at least 720 milligrams of calcium per day (45 grams of protein times 16 milligrams of calcium per gram of protein). A meat eater taking in 100 grams of protein each day needs at least 1,600 milligrams of calcium to compensate for the amount of calcium that will be lost due to a high protein intake.

But that's not all. Sodium also has a dramatic effect on calcium losses, and that's a problem for vegetarians and nonvegetarians alike.

Table salt and processed foods such as cake mixes, commercial baked goods, frozen entrées, chips and snack foods, canned goods, and condiments are all loaded with sodium. So is fast food. We all need sodium, but we can get all that is necessary in what naturally occurs in unprocessed, whole foods. We don't have to add any salt or sodium at all. Read package labels and notice the amount of sodium a serving of each food contains. All of us should aim for limiting our sodium intakes to 2,000 milligrams per day.

SODIUM COUNT

To see how quickly the sodium content of common foods can add up, take a look at the list that follows.

Food	Sodium (mg)
Brownie (1 large)	175
Cheese pizza (1 small slice)	336
Chocolate cake (1 slice)	370
Chocolate chip cookies (3)	125
Corn chips (2 oz.)	358
French fries (medium serving)	240
Macaroni and cheese (1 cup)	1,000
Nachos with cheese (6-8)	816
Pancakes (3)	890
Popcorn (3 cups)	415
Potato chips (2 oz.)	338
Vegetable soup (1 cup)	990

WHAT ARE THE BEST SOURCES OF CALCIUM FOR VEGETARIANS? ➤ Cow's milk, of course, is a super-concentrated source of calcium. That makes sense—it's designed to transform a small calf into a strapping cow in several months' time. We humans, on the other hand, don't have nearly as much bone and teeth to build. That's why human babies drinking human breast milk are better off. Milk is species specific. People don't need milk from a cow.

CALCIUM COUNT

Some examples of foods rich in calcium are shown in the table below.

Food	Calcium (mg)
Almonds (2 tablespoons)	71
Bean burrito (Taco Bell)	139
Black beans (1 cup cooked)	46
Broccoli spears (½ cup boiled)	47
Chili (1 cup, vegetarian)	111
Collard greens (½ cup chopped, boiled)	179
Figs (10 dried)	269
Garbanzo beans (1 cup cooked)	80
Kale (½ cup chopped, steamed)	90
Orange juice (8 oz., calcium-fortified)	300
Soymilk (8 oz., calcium-fortified)	200
Swiss chard (½ cup chopped, boiled)	51
Tofu processed with calcium (½ cup firm)	238

Many vegetarians do include dairy products such as milk, cheese, and yogurt in their diets. If you choose to eat dairy products, be sure to select nonfat varieties. Two-thirds of the fat in dairy products is artery-clogging saturated fat, so keep that in mind and choose wisely. Buy nonfat milk, yogurt, and cheeses, or compare package labels and select those with the lowest saturated fat content.

On the other hand, if you choose not to eat dairy products, there are lots of other sources of calcium, and you don't have to eat a truckload of broccoli to get it!

You should, however, eat plenty of calcium-rich plant foods. It isn't hard to do unless your diet is dominated by junk foods that

What? No Milk Mustache?

Most people in the world drink little or no cow's milk because they can't digest it.

Babies produce an enzyme—lactase—that helps them digest lactose, the form of sugar found in mother's milk. As babies grow older, they slowly produce less lactase. By the time they are weaned, they have no more need for the enzyme and gradually lose the ability to produce it. That's natural, but it's also the reason that most human adults around the world (except for people of Northern European descent) can't digest milk. Lactose intolerance is a natural condition of adults who try to drink cow's milk. Since they can no longer digest the lactose in milk, the sugar passes from the stomach into the intestines undigested. The symptoms typically include gas, bloating, cramps, and diarrhea.

Most of the world's people are lactose intolerant to some extent. People of Northern European descent are an exception. They are thought to have inherited a genetic mutation that allows them to continue producing lactase into adulthood.

compete for space on your plate. Aim for three good-sized servings of calcium-rich plant foods daily—three quarters to one cup per serving.

THE NUTS AND BOLTS OF IRON ➤ Vegetarians are not more prone to iron deficiency than nonvegetarians, contrary to popular belief. In fact, vegetarians generally get more iron in their diets than do nonvegetarians.

It is true that iron from animal sources (called "heme iron") is very easily absorbed by the body, and that plant sources of iron (called "nonheme iron") are not as readily absorbed. This does not seem to be an issue for vegetarians who are well nourished. In fact, it may be advantageous for overall health.

Some parts of plant foods either inhibit or enhance the absorption of nonheme iron. It's as though there is a little tug-of-war going on in your body. Certain substances, such as the tannins in tea, inhibit the absorption of iron. On the other hand, other substances, including vitamin C, enhance the absorption of iron. Since fruits and vegetables are frequently high in vitamin C, vegetarian diets that are rich in fruits and vegetables usually contain plenty of vitamin C. The result is that most vegetarians absorb all the iron they need.

No Combining Necessary!

When it comes to protein in a vegetarian diet, the only combination you need to know is the one for your locker at the gym. Vegetarians from your parents' and grandparents' generations were taught that protein from plant foods was inferior to that from animal products. They were counseled that plant foods had to be eaten in certain combinations in order to make a "complete" protein. For example, people were told to eat rice with beans, bread with peanut butter, and pasta with cheese. It seemed that you needed a degree in chemistry to get it right. Many people drew the conclusion that it was tricky and risky to eat a vegetarian diet.

Today we know that it's not necessary for foods to be eaten with such precision. Plant foods contain all of the nutrients that you need to be healthy, and your body automatically takes care of any "combining" of nutrients that is necessary over the course of the day. Just remember the two keys to getting enough protein on a vegetarian diet: eat enough calories and a reasonable variety of foods.

Good sources of vitamin C include tomatoes, cabbage, citrus fruits and juices (such as oranges, grapefruits, lemons and limes), potatoes, green peppers, strawberries, kiwi, and many

15

others. You probably eat vitamin C-rich foods with your meals regularly and don't even realize it—tomato sauce on pasta, boiled potatoes with your veggie burger, coleslaw with a sandwich, and orange juice with your bowl of cereal in the morning.

SOME STRAIGHT TALK ABOUT VITAMIN B_{12} ➤ Our requirement for vitamin B_{12} is miniscule—a mere 2 micrograms per day (that's .002 grams). It may seem odd that anyone should have to worry about getting enough.

Most people don't have to worry. Vitamin B_{12} is widely available in all animal foods. Teen vegetarians who include eggs and dairy products in their diets also get plenty of vitamin B_{12}. The potential problem is for those who consume no animal products whatsoever. That's because as far as anyone now knows, plants contain no vitamin B_{12}.

IRON COUNT

Conveniently, many of the foods that are high in calcium are also high in iron. This table shows how much iron you get in various iron-rich foods.

Food	Iron (mg)
Almonds (2 tablespoons)	1.1
Apricots (10 dried halves)	1.7
Black beans (1 cup cooked)	3.6
Blackstrap molasses (1 tablespoon)	0.9
Bran flakes (⅔ cup)	8.1
Bread (1 slice whole wheat)	0.9
Broccoli spears (½ cup cooked)	0.6
Brussels sprouts (½ cup cooked)	0.9
Garbanzo beans (1 cup cooked)	4.7
Kale (½ cup cooked)	0.6
Oatmeal (1 cup cooked)	1.6
Prunes (10 dried)	2.1
Soybeans (½ cup green, cooked)	2.3
Swiss chard (½ cup cooked)	2.0
Tempeh (½ cup)	1.9
Tofu (raw, firm, ½ cup)	13.2

Ironing Out the Facts

Scientists now believe that too much iron from animal sources may increase the risk of coronary artery disease. Iron, a potent oxidant, converts cholesterol into a form that is more readily absorbed by the arteries. Plant foods, on the other hand, are rich in antioxidants that help arrest the damage caused by the oxidants to which our bodies are exposed. So, it's not only easy to get enough iron on a vegetarian diet, but it's healthier too.

Vitamin B_{12} is produced by microorganisms that exist all around us in the soil, in ponds and streams, and in the guts of animals, including humans. Since the vitamin is produced in animals, any animal product that you eat will contain vitamin B_{12}.

VITAMIN B_{12} IMPOSTERS

There are actually many forms of vitamin B_{12}. The form that humans need is called cyanocobalamin. Other forms of the vitamin are referred to as analogs, and they are inactive in humans. This is important to know, because analogs may compete for absorption with cyanocobalamin and promote a deficiency. For many years, certain vegetarian food products were touted as being good sources of vitamin B_{12}. It turns out that these foods contain mostly analogs of vitamin B_{12} and are not a reliable source of cyanocobalamin.

The vitamin B_{12} imposters include tempeh, miso, tamari, some brands of nutritional yeast (except Red Star's Vegetarian Support Formula, also known as T-6635+, which is fine), sea vegetables such as kombu, kelp, nori, spirulina, and other forms of algae, and bean sprouts. It's okay to eat these foods as long as you also have a reliable daily source of cyanocobalamin in your diet as well.

Fruits and vegetables, in their natural environment, harbor vitamin B_{12} in the soil that clings to their skins or peels. Most of us, however, buy produce that has been washed clean of any soil. Even our water is chlorinated for public health reasons, killing any bacteria that might otherwise be a source of vitamin B_{12}. In today's world, vegetarians who avoid all animal products have few remaining sources of vitamin B_{12}. Your body recycles some of its B_{12}, so it's okay if you miss a day. But it's a good idea for vegans and near vegans to try to include a reliable source of vitamin B_{12} in their diets daily. That way they are assured of having enough. It's not difficult to do.

RELIABLE SOURCES OF VITAMIN B_{12}

Fortified soymilk and rice milk
Fortified breakfast cereals
Red Star brand Vegetarian Support Formula Nutritional Yeast
Vitamin B_{12} supplements
Fortified meat substitutes such as many brands of veggie burgers

If you have any doubts about whether or not you are getting enough vitamin B_{12}, the best bet is to simply take a supplement. Many drug stores and natural foods stores carry vitamin B_{12} tablets that contain 50 micrograms of the vitamin or more. If you take 50 mcg of vitamin B_{12} (cyanocobalamin), your body will probably only absorb 2 mcg. That's plenty.

OTHER IMPORTANT NUTRIENTS

Dozens of other nutrients are also important to the health of teens and everyone else too. They include vitamin D, the B vitamins, zinc, and a whole long list of other vitamins and minerals, as well as beneficial phytochemicals that scientists are only now beginning to identify and research.

A WORD ABOUT FATS

Vegetarian diets tend to be lower in total fat as compared with nonvegetarian diets. That's a good thing, and it helps to explain why vegetarians often enjoy better health than nonvegetarians. Vegetarian diets are generally lower in saturated fat, which comes from animal products (meats and dairy products) as well as from a few plant sources, including palm and coconut oils and cocoa butter. Saturated fats raise your blood cholesterol level and increase your risk for heart disease. Meats, cheese, ice cream, sour cream, milk, and butter are high in saturated fat. You'll find palm oil, coconut oil, and cocoa butter in store-bought cakes, cookies, pies, and other desserts, as well as in candies and other junk foods. Though they may be vegetarian, they're still not good for your health.

Years ago, nutritionists counseled people to use margarine instead of butter, but today even that advice has changed. Now we know that margarine, which contains trans-fatty acids, has an even greater blood cholesterol raising effect than does animal fat. If you want to add fat to your food, it's best to use olive oil when possible. Olive oil is an example of a monounsaturated

KEYS TO YOUR HEALTH ◀

It isn't practical or necessary to precisely monitor your intake of all the various nutrients. That would be a full time job. Instead, rely on a few easy-to-remember keys to eating a well-planned vegetarian diet:

➡ Be sure you get enough calories to meet your energy needs.

➡ Eat a reasonable variety of foods, including fruits, vegetables, whole grains, legumes, seeds and nuts.

➡ Vegans and near vegans should have a reliable source of vitamin B_{12} in their diets.

➡ Limit junk foods and other empty-calorie foods.

fat—a form of fat found in some plant foods that seems to be better for health. Other examples include the fat found in avocados and peanuts.

In fact, some fat is necessary for good health. Your body has a need for what nutrition scientists call essential fatty acids, also known as omega-3 and omega-6 fatty acids. These are found in a wide variety of plant foods such as nuts, seeds, and soyfoods. Flax seeds and oil are especially rich sources of essential fatty acids. The bottom line: nutrition scientists are still learning about the effects that various forms of fat have on our health. For now, vegetarians should aim to get most of their fat from whole foods such as seeds and nuts and, when necessary, using a little olive or flax oil.

FOOD GROUPS AND FOOD SELECTION

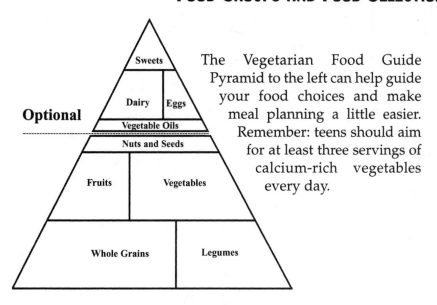

The Vegetarian Food Guide Pyramid to the left can help guide your food choices and make meal planning a little easier. Remember: teens should aim for at least three servings of calcium-rich vegetables every day.

Note: A reliable source of vitamin B_{12} should be included if no dairy or eggs are consumed.

For adults
- Aim for at least the minimum number of daily servings from each food group.
- Eat according to your appetite. If you need more calories than this meal guide suggests, then eat a greater number of servings from all of the groups to meet your energy needs.
- Vegans should be sure to include a reliable source of vitamin B_{12} in their diets.

*Source: Third International Congress on Vegetarian Nutrition and Loma Linda University; reprinted with permission.

Description of Food Groups and Recommendations for Food Selection

Food Group	Examples of Food Items	Recommendations
Whole grains	Grains: wheat, corn, oats, rice, millet, etc. Grain products: bread, pasta, tortillas	Select whole-wheat and whole-grain products.
Legumes	Beans and peas: soy, pinto, kidney, navy, limas, peas, lentils, garbanzos. Soy and soy products, tofu, soy drinks, texturized protein foods	Select soy-based milk alternatives fortified with calcium, vitamin D, and vitamin B_{12}.
Vegetables	All vegetables	Emphasize leafy green and yellow vegetables. Eat both cooked and raw.
Fruits	All fruits	Emphasize whole fruits rather than juice.
Nuts and seeds	Nuts: almonds, walnuts, peanuts, etc. Seeds: pumpkin, squash, sunflower, etc. Butters: peanut, almond, sesame (tahini).	Eat raw, dry-roasted, or in foods rather than deep-fried.
Vegetable oils	Plant oils: canola, corn, olive, etc.	Emphasize those high in monounsaturates such as olive, sesame, and canola. Limit tropical oils (coconut, palm kernel, palm oil). Avoid hydrogenated fats.
Milk and dairy	Milk, yogurt, cheese	Emphasize nonfat and low-fat products. If dairy is avoided, must ensure adequate, reliable sources of calcium and vitamin D.
Eggs		Limit eggs or use egg whites only.
Sweets	Honey, syrup (molasses, maple, carob), sugar, sweeteners, jams, jellies, etc.	Eat in moderation.
Vitamin B_{12}	Dietary supplement of fortified foods	A reliable source of B_{12} (cobalamin) should be included if dairy and eggs are avoided.

SURVIVAL IN THE SCHOOL LUNCH TRENCHES 101

Despite valiant efforts by nutrition advocates over the past several years (and the never ending complaints from students), the federal school lunch program is still a long way from serving healthful meals. To be fair to schools and food service personnel, it should be pointed out that the issues and challenges facing school meal programs—both breakfast and lunch—are complex. Radical changes are not likely to happen overnight. As a result, you are not likely to get a vegetarian meal at school anytime soon. If you are vegan, the choices will be even slimmer.

BAG IT! ➤ If you're serious about being a vegetarian at school and want a decent lunch, you'll most likely have to fend for yourself. This doesn't have to be hard, but you will need to be a little organized.

Supplement school food with food from home. Look at the school menu ahead of time and see if there are days on which you can eat the entrée or side dishes. On those days, take a couple of pieces of fresh fruit from home, a juice box, a muffin or other bread.

Circumstances are different at different schools, and some schools may have an easier time than others in accommodating your needs as a vegetarian. Consider sitting down with your school food service director and discussing your options. Listen carefully and be ready to offer some suggestions or practical solutions to the problem.

Lunchbox Winners

Hummus and peanut butter are good standbys for sandwich fillings, and they don't require refrigeration for the few hours they're in your locker before lunchtime.

Try muffins, bagels, juice boxes, carrot and celery sticks with salsa or hummus to dip into, and fresh fruit of all kinds (especially fruit that is in season).

If you have access to a microwave oven, take soup cups and hot cereal cups (add boiling water, stir, wait five minutes, eat).

Don't forget about leftovers from last night's dinner.

WEIGHT CONTROL & EXERCISE

Nationally, we are facing an epidemic of overweight. Though the stereotype is that teen girls want to lose weight and the guys want to gain it (in all the right places, of course), obesity is a problem for both sexes and all ages today.

If your diet is the cause of your excess weight, the problem is likely to be too much junk food—chips, soft drinks, candy bars (including sports bars and granola bars), fast food, and other sweets and greasy foods. What can you do?

There's no other way around it than to—

- ✓ Replace the junk with fresh fruit, hefty portions of vegetables, more beans and whole grains in place of refined and processed foods.
- ✓ Reach for an orange after school rather than a bag of chips or a handful of cookies.
- ✓ Reduce your portions at mealtime.
- ✓ Keep healthy snacks in your backpack or purse so that you'll have something good on hand when hunger strikes or you need a quick energy boost. Fresh fruit, bagels, small bags of dried fruit, and juice boxes are portable and nutritious.

It may take a little while to adjust to new eating habits, but you'll feel better when you do.

Do Vegetarians Have Eating Disorders?

Eating disorders such as anorexia nervosa (self starvation) and bulimia (binge and purge) are more common in teen girls than in teen boys or adults. However, there is no cause-and-effect relationship between vegetarian diets and eating disorders. Going vegetarian doesn't create an eating disorder. Some anorexics do stop eating meat, but it's usually due to changes in the way meats taste to them, or it may be a way to justify their restrictive eating style to others. Eating disorders have psychological origins. People with eating disorders need psychiatric or psychological counseling.

If you're not active, find something active you like to do, grab a friend and get going.

Look at your level of physical activity. Make exercise a part of your daily life—walk or bike to get around. Aerobic dance classes and weight training are great ways of improving your heart function as well as building strength. Burning calories regularly through physical activity will help you lose pounds. If going to the gym bores you, then find something you do like to do. Vary your activities. If it's summertime, get active canoeing and kayaking, inline skating, swimming, hiking, and bike riding. In the cold months, go cross country skiing, walking, or skating. Figure out what appeals to you and do it.

TEEN ATHLETES ➤ If you are involved in athletics, you probably hear a lot of advice from coaches, friends, teachers, magazines, and books about what you should eat for optimal performance and to stay healthy. Some sources will tell you that you need more of certain nutrients—particularly protein—if you engage in vigorous sports regularly.

It's important to put this matter in perspective. It's true that certain athletes—namely those who are regularly engaged in very strenuous activity—have a slightly increased need for protein. Whereas most people should aim for approximately 0.8 grams of protein per kilogram of body weight, elite athletes need about 1.0 gram of protein per kilogram of body weight. However, if you are very physically active, you need more calories too. Those extra calories you take in can easily cover your increased need for protein and other nutrients, provided you are eating wholesome foods and not loading up on junk. There is no need for protein powders and no need to consciously increase your intake of specific nutrients. Just eat larger servings at mealtime and include wholesome between meal snacks such as bagels, nonfat yogurt, sandwiches, cereal, fresh fruit, popcorn, bean burritos, and leftovers from dinner the day before.

> ### SAFE & HEALTHY WEIGHT GAIN TIPS
>
> ✗ Smoothies and juice blends are easy to whip up and drink and can add substantial calories to your diet.
> ✗ Replace some lower calorie foods such as lettuce salad, broth soups, and low calorie vegetables (green beans, beets, carrots) with starchier, higher calorie foods such as potatoes, beans, hearty soups, and vegetarian chili.
> ✗ Eat more frequent snacks.

It can't be emphasized enough—the greatest challenge for most teens, vegetarian or not, is limiting the empty calorie foods that provide calories and excess fat and sodium at the expense of vital nutrients.

BULKING UP THE RIGHT WAY ➤ If you happen to be a teen guy who wants to gain weight, do it wisely. Downing protein powders is not the way to bulk up. All you'll do is tax your kidneys and your wallet. Instead, eat larger portions of the good stuff at mealtime—vegetables, grains, beans, and fruit.

Adding weight-bearing exercise will also help you build muscle, and therefore weight, within limits. Remember that some people are naturally leaner than others. Try to keep a realistic perspective with regards to your physique. Gaining weight by adding layers of fat tissue is probably not what you want to do.

HANDLING THE SOCIAL SIDE

WHAT HAPPENS WHEN MEAT-AND-POTATOES MEETS VEGGIE BURGER DELUXE, HOLD THE CHEESE?

Now that you know how to eat right on a vegetarian diet, the next challenge is to educate your nonvegetarian family and friends and boost their confidence in your ability to fare well on a diet that excludes meat and possibly other animal products. There is no need to try to convert them. Just show them that you're fine.

BE A ROLE MODEL ➤ Show people that you really do like broccoli and sweet potatoes. Let them see you eating nutritious meals on a regular basis and enjoying your food. Let them see the variety in your daily meals as well as how appealing well-prepared, nutritious foods can be. Vegetarian meals are typically colorful and diverse, incorporating traditional foods from other cultures. It's hard not to be attracted to vegetarian meals. Even nonvegetarians respond to the rich aromas, colors, flavors, textures, and creative combinations of ingredients in vegetarian cuisines.

BE POSITIVE ➤ And confident. People will respond. A positive, can-do attitude instills confidence in others and can help generate support for your lifestyle. Resist the temptation to pressure others to make the switch themselves, however. They probably don't want to hear it. The way that you'll be most successful in influencing others is to simply be who you are and set an example. Some day they may be ready to change their own lifestyles, and you'll be there to offer support.

Resist the temptation to become the diet police. It bears repeating: people do not want to be pestered into changing their eating habits. They may know that a vegetarian diet is healthier,

 Nonvegetarians Need Love Too!

Here are some important considerations that can help you be more tolerant when talking with nonvegetarians.

❧ Meat and dairy products often have great significance and a variety of meanings according to the culture that a person comes from.

❧ People often develop strong emotional associations to foods and eating habits learned in childhood. Challenging these habits can actually be threatening to the way some people feel about themselves.

❧ If you're vegetarian because you're sensitive about the feelings of anonymous animals, you certainly don't want to show any less consideration for the feelings and values of the humans around you.

❧ Nonvegetarians have their own lives, and you are asking them to be flexible in tolerating your beliefs. It's only fair for you to be equally tolerant of their chosen lifestyle.

and they may understand that it's better for the environment. They still may not be ready to commit to change. If you press, you may alienate people. Influence by your example. You are much more likely to be effective that way and to preserve relationships.

HELP OUT WITH FAMILY MEALS ➤ If your family eats meals together, get involved in meal planning. Your parents will thank you for it. You may even find that you spark everyone's interest in food and nutrition.

Lend a hand with weekly grocery shopping, and help prepare meals. Experiment with recipes from vegetarian cookbooks such as this one, and give everyone a chance to choose one they like.

EXPERIMENT WITH FOOD ➤ Foster the spirit of adventure in your family by experimenting with foods from other cultures or unusual fruits and vegetables.

You'll find a few bombs along the way, but you'll also discover some new favorites. It's all part of the process of trying new things, and that's what life is all about!

START A KITCHEN GARDEN ➤ You don't need much space to nurture a kitchen garden. It can be a few terra cotta pots of tomatoes and herbs or a patch of land outside your house or apartment. Growing some of your own foods is fun and rewarding, and it may help family members take an interest.

VEGETARIANISM IN THE REAL WORLD

Being the only vegetarian in your family brings challenges, but being a vegetarian outside your home brings a whole different set. Though vegetarianism is becoming more mainstream, you are still likely to eat very differently than most of the people you hang out with. That means that you will have to do most of the adapting when it comes to handling situations involving food.

Some of the most common issues facing vegetarian teens aren't all that difficult to deal with if you just think them through ahead of time.

DATING ➤ It's easy when you're both vegetarian. The only decision you'll have to make when you go out to eat is whether you want Mexican or Thai. However, if your date is not a vegetarian, it's probably best to broach the subject of food early on to head off an awkward situation later.

There's no need to make a big deal out of being a vegetarian, though. It doesn't have to be your entire identity. Be matter of fact about your food preferences. If someone asks you out to dinner, casually mention that you are a vegetarian but that you can find something to eat in most any restaurant. Hopefully, your date will follow up with some suggestions for restaurants that serve a range of foods so that you will have choices. Ethnic restaurants such as Chinese, Thai, Mexican, Italian, Indian, and Middle Eastern are often a good bet.

If you get into a discussion about food, emphasize all of the foods that you *do* eat. The truth is, you probably have more variety in your diet than do nonvegetarians. Give some specific examples of foods that you eat regularly, such as bean burritos,

Chinese stir-fry, Italian pasta dishes, lentil soup, nachos, hummus with pita bread, and so on.

EATING AT SOMEONE'S HOME ➤ It's always best to let your host know right away that you are a vegetarian. You don't want anyone to go to the trouble of fixing something that you couldn't eat. People really feel badly when they go to serve you a big steak only to find out that you won't eat it. Your host wants you to enjoy your meal, so when you get the invitation, say thanks and accept, but also go ahead and mention that you are a vegetarian. Explain precisely what you eat and what you don't eat. You can let your host know that he or she doesn't have to go out of the way to make you something special.

Your host may suggest a dish such as spaghetti or lasagne, something that they are familiar with and that might be acceptable to you. Feel free to toss out other ideas that typically appeal to everyone, such as red beans and rice or chili (vegetarian) and cornbread. Offer to bring a dish to share with everyone, and note that with vegetables, salad, bread, and other side dishes you are certain to have plenty to eat.

> ## OTHER TIPS FOR EATING OUT
>
> - Look at the side dishes offered with entrees. Pick out some items that sound good and create your own "vegetarian plate."
>
> - Put together a meal from the appetizer section of the menu.
>
> - Choose ethnic restaurants that generally offer several vegetable options. Indian, Mexican, Italian, Chinese, Thai, Ethiopian, and Middle Eastern restaurants are good bets.
>
> - Baked potatoes are often huge and filling. A baked potato and a trip to the salad bar may be all the food you want or need.
>
> - If pasta is on the menu, you're all set. Ask for pasta with garlic and olive oil tossed with steamed, fresh vegetables. Pasta with marinara sauce or pesto is also good.
>
> - Ask your waitperson for a suggestion if a vegetarian option isn't visible on the menu.

RESTAURANT SURVIVAL ➤ It's getting easier and easier to find vegetarian options on restaurant menus. Many family restaurants serve veggie burgers, and most better restaurants offer at least one or two vegetarian entrees, often a pasta dish or a vegetable plate. Restaurants that make food to order are usually happy to alter a menu item to make it vegetarian. A Rueben sandwich, for instance, can be made without the corned beef. A shrimp stir-fry can be made with vegetables and rice, hold the shrimp.

For a list of vegetarian restaurants in your city, check the Vegetarian Resource Group's web site at www.vrg.org. The organization also continually updates a book that lists natural foods and vegetarian restaurants across the country: *Vegetarian Journal's Guide to Natural Food Restaurants in the U.S. and Canada* (Avery Publishing Group, Garden City Park, NY.) And see the websites and other resources listed in the back of this book.

GETTING INVOLVED

There are lots of ways to get connected with the wider vegetarian world that are interesting and fun. You'll gain valuable information and experience along the way.

CONNECT WITH LOCAL VEGETARIAN GROUPS ➤ If you live in a mid sized or big city, it's likely to have a local vegetarian society. If you live in a small town, don't give up hope until you've checked around. It only takes one interested person to get a group started. Local vegetarian organizations are thriving in some of the most unlikely places.

Some local vegetarian organizations are affiliated with churches like the Seventh-day Adventist church, and some are affiliated with other philosophical, environmental, or political movements or groups. Many organizations are run by individuals who simply want to connect with other vegetarians, whatever their political or philosophical views. The organizations usually meet once a month in such locations as an individual member's home, a church community room, or a room in the local library or other public place. Some groups even meet at restaurants.

No Local Vegetarian Group? Start Your Own

The Vegetarian Resource Group has materials to help you organize your own local group. Contact the organization via email at vrg@vrg.org, or call 1-410-366-VEGE (1-410-366-8343).

Some groups publish newsletters, and many sponsor special meetings or events around particular holidays or observances, such as Thanksgiving, World Vegetarian Day (October 1st), and the Fourth of July.

Find a vegetarian organization in your area by checking the phone book, asking other vegetarians or the manager of a natural foods store, inquiring at a Seventh-day Adventist Church or a Unitarian Universalist Church, or by calling the Vegetarian Resource Group to see if the staff knows of a group in your area. You can also check your local newspaper or alternative press paper for a mention of a vegetarian society meeting. Many college and university campuses also host vegetarian groups.

> **If You Need Individualized Help**
>
> If you have specific concerns or questions and need individualized assistance with planning or evaluating your diet, consult a registered dietitian.
>
> The American Dietetic Association runs a referral service that can locate a registered dietitian familiar with vegetarian or vegan diets in your area. Call the ADA toll-free at 1-800-366-1655 and ask them for a referral.

CHECK OUT THE NATIONAL GROUPS ➤ National vegetarian organizations can also be a source of events and activities in which you might participate. Some sponsor conferences and other events such as special programs that draw vegetarians and other interested individuals from around the country and around the world. See the list of national organizations with websites and contact information on pages 152-153.

READ ALL ABOUT IT! ➤ If you'd like to see more info in print, see our list of books and magazines on pages 152-153.

Suzanne Havala, MS, RD, LDN, FADA

If you're looking for a quick lunch you can make at home, the vegetarian possibilities are limitless. There are all sorts of vegetarian soup and sandwich choices. One of my favorite quick-and-hearty soups can be found at most supermarkets: Progresso's Lentil Soup. It's one of the few commercial bean soups that's completely vegetarian. It will really round out a meal and tastes great.

As far as sandwiches go, there's a vegetarian substitute for any type of deli slice you can imagine: bologna, ham, chicken, turkey, pastrami, Canadian bacon, you name it. And there's a growing variety of dairy-free sliced cheeses you can use to make a great veggie sub. Worthington and Loma Linda make a number of canned and frozen meat substitutes that work really well in sandwiches as well as main dishes, especially Worthington's tuna substitute.

If you're whipping up something for you and your friends, you can find boxed instant soup mixes and canned vegetarian chilis in your natural foods store. Add some fresh or frozen vegetables to packaged vegetarian ramen soup mix, along with some cubed tofu or textured soy crumbles, for a quick, complete meal.

If you like Mexican food, keep some canned beans or instant bean mixes on hand (the just-add-water-and-mix kind). Tortillas keep well in the freezer and reheat quickly on a dry, hot griddle. All you need is the salsa, diced tomatoes, shredded soy cheese, and chopped lettuce. If you get cravings for Chinese, keep a supply of canned Chinese vegetables, bean sprouts, and water chestnuts handy. Heat and mix with tofu cubes, and eat over instant brown rice.

There are dozens of vegetarian burgers and hot dogs available. These are great for taking to picnics, barbeques, and other outdoor get-togethers. Your nonveggie friends will be surprised how delicious they are.

If pasta is your thing, there are now many tasty, instant pasta meals, full of good-for-you ingredients, that you can buy at natural food stores. For vegans, there is even a brand of dairy-free "cheese" and pasta meals that you prepare just like commercial packaged macaroni and cheese.

Quick Lunch Ideas

Don't stop with peanut butter—explore the many other yummy nut butters, like almond and cashew butters and tahini (from sesame seeds). Try spreads and dips like hummus, apple butter, and multi-flavored soy "cream cheese" for variety.

Another option is a complete vegetarian meal, either frozen or in a vacuum package you can store on your pantry shelf. Whether your idea of a great meal is lasagne, unturkey with gravy and mashed potatoes, or Chinese food, it's out there.

For lunches at school or work, when you may only have a microwave available, instant meal and/or soup cups are inexpensive, quick, and tasty. There's about every sort of food combination you can think of: macaroni and cheese, Mexican food, split pea soup, Thai noodles, stews and chili, even rice pudding! Frozen pita pockets and veggie wraps are becoming more popular and are easy and quick to heat in the microwave. You can usually find frozen, all-vegetarian bean burritos in the frozen food section of large supermarkets.

Don't forget leftovers. Build up your supply of plastic containers so you can make a big dinner and enjoy the leftovers for lunch over the next few days. (Reheat on paper plates if you can, as microwaving plastics is not always harmless.)

Quick Snack Ideas

Sure, potato chips are vegetarian, . . . but you can do better than that! We all eat a little junk food now and again, but save some room for snacks that are good for you too. You'll find they're more satisfying in the long run and keep you from getting hungry before the next meal. Instead of chips, go for pretzels; they're a lot lower in calories. Popcorn's a quick snack you can feel good about eating a lot of (if you can hold off drowning it in butter). Try topping it with chili powder, garlic powder, nondairy Parmesan cheese, or nutritional yeast. (Or if you're a hot sauce freak, sprinkle with Tabasco sauce!)

A favorite high-protein snack among vegetarians and vegans is vegetarian jerky. It comes in lots of flavors and is so good it's positively addictive. Made from all-soy or a combination of soy, seitan, and/or tofu, veggie jerky won't crumble to pieces in your backpack or melt in your purse, so it makes great travel or camping food. Something else you might try is vegetarian pâté. It makes a good sandwich spread, vegetable dip, or partner for crackers. And don't forget bean dips. You can spice up instant refried beans with your favorite salsa. For something different, try this with instant black beans.

If you'd rather not eat dairy products, make party dips with soy sour cream or cream cheese. If you have a passion for baked potatoes, bake several at a time and store extra in the freezer. You can defrost them in the microwave and top with soy sour cream and vegetarian bacon bits. There are also nondairy cheese sauces available now; just add your favorite salsa for a great tortilla chip dip. The choices keep getting better and more plentiful; you can get several types of soy yogurt now, as well as instant soy puddings and pudding cups.

Nuts are delicious—the good news is we now know how good they are for you. Begin a life-long habit of including some in your meals or snacks every day. Almonds are a good source of calcium, walnuts contain a type of essential fatty acid that is not easy to get from other foods, and pumpkin seeds are high in zinc. Just know your limits—although nuts and seeds contain a lot of good fats, they are high in calories.

If you're a vegetarian athlete or enjoy hiking, rock climbing, biking, or other endurance sports, you might actually need high-calorie snack foods to help keep you going between meals. Trail mixes with different combinations of dried fruits and nuts or protein bars (especially one of the delicious soy protein bars now available) are good choices.

As for sweets, try to work as much fruit into your sweet treats as you can. You can make vegetarian gelatins in delicious fruit flavors and layer them with chopped fresh fruit and vegetarian whipped topping to make parfaits that look as delicious as ice cream sundaes. Instant hot cereal cups can also satisfy the urge for something sweet, whether or not it's time for breakfast. Keep some frozen blueberries and strawberries around to add to hot cereals and desserts. Make it a point always to have your favorite fresh fruit around: apples, bananas, oranges, grapes— eat more fruit!

If you don't have a handy local food outlet that sells these items, you can order many of them from the mail order sources listed on page 153.

smoothies

Dark Cherry Frappe

Cinnamon Silence Smoothie

Lemonade or Limeade

Mango Lassi

Chunky Monkey Shake

Mulled Cider

Piña Colada Smoothie

Strawberry Shake

Tuscon Tonic

Pima Pear Whip

Wilcox Apple Pie Shake

Tahitian Surprise Tropical Breakfast Smoothie

Orange Peach Smoothie

Avo-Banana Whip

Rainbow's End Smoothie

Cookies and Cream Frappe

Key Lime Whip

Date Shake

Vegan Holiday Nog

Rich Fruit Shake

Orange Dream

Banana Cappucino Froth

Ironman Shake

and shakes

Dark Cherry Frappe

Makes 2 servings

Hungry? Creatively frustrated? In a hurry? Satisfy all your needs. Ahhh, Smoothie!

½ cup pitted or frozen cherries

1 frozen banana

1 cup raw, unfiltered apple juice

1 tablespoon carob powder

2 cherries with stems, for garnish

Blend all the ingredients, except the cherries, until smooth. Serve, garnished with the cherries. Enjoy!

Per serving: Calories 155, Protein 1 g,
Fat 0 g, Carbohydrates 36 g

Cinnamon Silence Smoothie

Makes 2 servings

The silence comes from being so busy savoring this rich, spicy treat that you forget to talk. This drink is a baby-sitter's friend!

2 frozen bananas

1 cup raw, unfiltered apple juice

¼ teaspoon pure vanilla

Pinch of ground cinnamon

2 cinnamon sticks, for garnish

Blend all the ingredients, except the cinnamon sticks, until smooth. Serve, garnished with the cinnamon sticks. Enjoy!

Per serving: Calories 163, Protein 1 g,
Fat 0 g, Carbohydrates 38 g

Lemonade or Limeade

Makes 8 servings

"When life gives you lemons, make lemonade."—Unknown
Try this with rice syrup or, even, pure maple syrup.

1 cup liquid sweetener, or to taste

2 quarts cold water

Juice of 6 lemons

Juice of 2 limes

Juice of 1 orange (optional)

In a large pot, mix the sweetener and water, and cook slowly until the sweetener is completely dissolved. Add the fruit juices and mix well. Refrigerate or add ice cubes. (If the mixture is too hot, ice cubes will melt and the drink may become too weak.) Serve garnished with a slice of lime and/or a sprig of mint. Enjoy!

Per serving: Calories 91, Protein 1 g,
Fat 0 g, Carbohydrates 22 g

Variations

Try with all lemons, all limes (remember, limes are smaller, you'll have to use more), more oranges, or substitute grapefruits or tangerines.

Substitute pure prickly pear fruit juice for all or part of the lemons. If using a sweetened prickly pear syrup, cut back on the amount of other sweetener to compensate.

Mango Lassi

Makes 2 servings

One of the best reasons to dine at Indian restaurants is to enjoy a smooth, creamy mango lassi. Simple and delicious, sip slowly and savor the refreshing coolness.

2 fresh, ripe mangoes, peeled, seeded, and chopped, or 1 cup dried mango, soaked until soft and chopped into small pieces

2 tablespoons sucanat or rapadura sugar

2 cups soy yogurt

1 tablespoon rosewater, or juice of 1 lime (optional)

2 to 3 ice cubes (optional)

Blend all the ingredients together well, and serve. Enjoy!

Per serving Calories 274, Protein 6 g,
Fat 5 g, Carbohydrates 38 g

 *ariations*

Perhaps not quite a traditional lassi but delicious anyway, try adding a few fresh strawberries or pineapple chunks, pineapple or orange juice, or a ripe banana.

Add a small dash of vanilla extract.

Alright, go completely decadent if you like, and add a scoop of nondairy ice cream. Or fruit sorbet.

Chunky Monkey Shake

Makes 2 servings

In a rut? If you're tired of the same-old same-old, here's some quick, sweet, and nutritious ideas to help you get unstuck.

2 cups soymilk or rice milk

2 ripe bananas (see note below)

4 tablespoons roasted cashews (see note below)

**2 tablespoons roasted carob powder plus
2 tablespoons sucanat, or maple syrup, or ¼ cup
malt-sweetened vegan carob chips**

In an electric blender, blend all the ingredients together until smooth and creamy. Serve garnished with a mint leaf.

Per serving: Calories 365, Protein 9 g,
Fat 13 g, Carbohydrates 52 g

Notes: You can put those very ripe bananas (you know, when they get brown or black) in the freezer, peel intact, and save them for banana bread or smoothies like this. Either thaw a banana and use in your recipe, or for a smoothie, place the banana in a dish of hot water for about 30 seconds just until the peel becomes soft enough to remove. Blend the frozen banana.

It's very simple to roast raw cashews in a dry, heavy skillet (cast-iron works well) over medium. heat, stirring often, until golden brown. These taste better than buying already-roasted cashews.

 *ariations*

Add a scoop or two of nondairy frozen dessert.

Try fresh or frozen fruit in place of the carob—strawberries, raspberries, peaches, etc.

You can, of course, substitute sweetened chocolate or cocoa in place of the carob.

Mulled Cider

Makes 1 gallon

Wonderfully warming, this spicy version of hot cider will brighten any house with delightful aromas. Have a party and share the holidays over big mugs of steaming mulled cider.

Mulling Spices

2 tablespoons ground cinnamon

1 teaspoon ground nutmeg

¼ teaspoon ground ginger

Pinch of ground cloves

1 gallon apple cider or unfiltered apple juice

Place the ground spices in a muslin tea bag, and put the bag in the cider. Gently and slowly heat the cider or juice and mulling spices together in a crockpot or large soup pot. Do not boil the cider, and keep it hot while serving. When finished mulling the cider, discard the spices into your compost, and wash the bag to re-use.

Per cup: Calories 116, Protein 0 g, Fat 0 g, Carbohydrates 28 g

Tips and Variations

If you do not have a muslin tea bag, you may use a tea ball. The only problem is that the ground spices will fall through the holes in the tea ball. Use whole or cracked spices instead: about 4 to 6 cinnamon sticks, ½ cracked nutmeg, 2 to 3 whole cloves, and a little ginger juice. (Grate fresh ginger root and squeeze in the palm of your hand to make juice.)

Add any of the following for subtle variations in flavor: fresh or dried orange peel, star anise, sassafras, sarsaparilla, or allspice.

Float a few extra cinnamon sticks or some chopped dried apples in the mulling juice as a garnish.

Piña Colada Smoothie

Makes 8 servings

Sip this refreshing drink with your eyes closed, and you'll almost feel the sea breezes of the Mexican coast.

2 cups pineapple juice

2 cups coconut milk

1 cup sucanat

2 cups soymilk or rice milk

1 teaspoon pure vanilla

2 cups crushed ice

Blend all the ingredients well, and serve garnished with a mint leaf.

Per 2 servings: Calories 589, Protein 5 g,
Fat 23 g, Carbohydrates 32 g

Strawberry Shake

Makes 4 servings

1 cup fresh or frozen strawberries

2 cups soymilk or nut milk

½ cup powdered soymilk

1 cup crushed ice (if using fresh fruit)

Blend all the ingredients well. Garnish with a fresh strawberry or a mint leaf, and have a flavorful good time!

Per serving: Calories 108, Protein 11 g,
Fat 3 g, Carbohydrates 10 g

Tucson Tonic

Makes 2 servings

What a wonderful, simple way to brighten up your morning!

Juice of 4 oranges (1 cup juice)
1 large mango, peeled and seed removed
½ cup raw, unfiltered apple juice
2 orange slices, for garnish

Blend all the ingredients, except the orange slices, until smooth and frothy. Garnish with the orange slices, serve, and enjoy!

Per serving: Calories 161, Protein 1 g,
Fat 0 g, Carbohydrates 38 g

Pima Pear Whip

Makes 2 servings

Refreshing and light, perfect for a hot summer day!

4 very ripe pears
¼ cup raw, unfiltered apple juice
2 tablespoons lemon juice
4 ice cubes
2 strawberries, for garnish

Blend all the ingredients, except the strawberries, until smooth and frothy. Serve garnished with the fresh strawberries for a totally enjoyable treat!

Per serving: Calories 217, Protein 1 g,
Fat 0 g, Carbohydrates 50 g

Wilcox Apple Pie Shake

Makes 2 servings

There are lots of nondairy milks available today—soymilk, rice milk, oat milk, almond milk, and some combinations. Many of them are vitamin fortified. Try a few to find some that you like. (Give the rejects to your dog or cat.)

2 large apples, cored, peeled or not

1 cup nondairy yogurt

1 cup any nondairy milk

2 tablespoons maple syrup

1 teaspoon cinnamon

Pinch of nutmeg

Pinch of cloves

Blend all the ingredients until smooth. Pour into tall glasses and garnish with a cinnamon stick. Slurp and enjoy!

Per serving: Calories 210, Protein 6 g,
Fat 5 g, Carbohydrates 36 g

Variations

Substitute frozen nondairy yogurt or other frozen dessert for the yogurt.

Substitute granulated cane juice crystals for the maple syrup.

Sprinkle the top lightly with graham cracker crumbs just before serving.

For extra nutrition, you might add 1 tablespoon soy protein powder to this or any other shake.

Tahitian Sunrise Tropical
Breakfast Smoothie

Makes 4 servings

What a great way to wake up! See for yourself why coconut milk is the beverage of choice in the Caribbean and other tropical locales.

2 fresh, ripe mangoes,* peeled and chopped

1 cup fresh orange juice

1 cup fresh or canned coconut milk

Juice of 1 lime

1 tablespoon flaxseed oil (optional)

Blend all the ingredients well, and serve in a tall glass for you and your guests to enjoy.

Per 2 servings: Calories 433, Protein 3 g,
Fat 22 g, Carbohydrates 49 g

*When fresh mangoes are out of season or hard to obtain, cut dried mango into small pieces and soak in water for ½ hour to hydrate. One-half cup of soaked dried mango will equal 1 fresh mango.

Variations

Substitute fresh pineapple for the mango.

Substitute yogurt for the coconut milk.

Add a handful of raw cashews before blending.

Orange Peach Smoothie

Makes 2 servings

This sweet, refreshing smoothie can be made with either fresh or frozen peaches. I don't like to remove the peel, but if you don't like the fuzziness, go ahead and peel the peach. The cashews add a smooth richness.

1 cup orange juice

½ cup cashews

2 large or 3 small peaches, seeded

2 tablespoons protein powder (optional)

Blend the orange juice and cashews until very smooth. Add the rest of the ingredients, and blend again. Serve in a tall glass and enjoy!

Per serving: Calories 310, Protein 6 g,
Fat 16 g, Carbohydrates 34 g

ariations

Substitute papaya juice for all or part of the orange juice.

Soak ½ cup almonds in distilled water for 2 days, and use in place of cashews. You'll be surprised what the soaking does for the flavor and digestibility of the almonds.

Avo-Banana Whip

Makes 2 servings

This unusual smoothie is delicious and packed with nutrients. The kiwi and strawberries add a nice sweet-tart flavor that harmonizes well with the avocado and bananas.

1 large avocado, peeled and seeded

2 frozen bananas

1 kiwi, peeled

½ cup frozen strawberries

1 cup apple juice or kefir (liquid yogurt)

Juice of 1 lime (optional)

2 tablespoons brown rice syrup

Blend all the ingredients together until smooth. Serve in a tall glass for maximum enjoyment!

Per serving: Calories 432, Protein 4 g, Fat 13 g, Carbohydrates 74 g

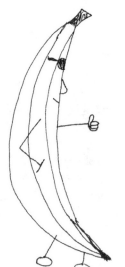

Rainbow's End Smoothie

Makes 2 servings

Sweet and spicy, this golden smoothie is a real treasure.

½ cup strong-brewed chai tea

1 fresh mango, peeled and seeded, or soaked
  dried mango*

1 scoop peach or orange sorbet

1 cup orange juice

Blend all the ingredients well, and serve in a frosted glass.

*When fresh mangoes are out of season or hard to obtain, cut dried
mango into small pieces and soak in water for ½ hour to hydrate.
One-half cup of soaked dried mango will equal 1 fresh mango.*

Per serving: Calories 154, Protein 1 g,
Fat 0 g, Carbohydrates 36 g

Cookies and Cream Frappe

Makes 2 servings

Reward yourself for something! Anything!

4 or 5 of your favorite cookies

2 frozen bananas

2 scoops nondairy frozen dessert

1 cup nondairy milk

Blend all the ingredients well, and serve in a tall glass.
You'll need a spoon for this one!

Per serving: Calories 352, Protein 9 g,
Fat 9 g, Carbohydrates 57 g

Key Lime Whip

Makes 2 servings

This rich drink is soooo refreshing on a hot summer day after you've finished the chores.

⅓ cup lime juice

1 (12.3-ounce) package firm silken tofu

1 cup nondairy milk or fresh coconut milk

⅓ cup sugar or dehydrated sugar cane juice sweetener

Dash of pure vanilla (optional)

Whip all the ingredients together well in a blender, and serve in a tall, frosted glass. Garnish with a lime twist and a sprig of fresh mint for extra color and flavor.

Per serving: Calories 275, Protein 15 g,
Fat 7 g, Carbohydrates 39 g

Date Shake

Makes 4 servings

Use medjool or honey dates, rather than those dried dates that you find in the produce department of the supermarket around the holidays.

3 cups nondairy milk

9 or 10 large pitted dates

3 tablespoons chopped almonds

Blend all the ingredients well. Garnish with a dash of cinnamon or nutmeg, if you so desire.

Per serving: Calories 156, Protein 6 g,
Fat 7 g, Carbohydrates 18 g

Vegan Holiday Nog

Makes 8 servings

Here's a rich eggless, dairyless variation of a holiday tradition. Keep in mind that it's still not low fat, although there is no cholesterol and less saturated fat than regular egg nog.

4 (12.3-ounce) packages silken firm tofu

4 cups soymilk or rice milk

½ cup sucanat, or maple syrup

½ cup canola oil

½ teaspoon nutmeg

¼ teaspoon cinnamon

1 teaspoon pure vanilla extract

¼ teaspoon butterscotch flavoring (optional)

Blend all the ingredients well until frothy, and chill for 15 to 30 minutes. Serve with a cinnamon stick, and make any day a holiday!

Per 2 servings: Calories 492, Protein 12 g, Fat 33 g, Carbohydrates 11 g

Rich Fruit Shake

Makes 4 servings

4 (12.3-ounce) packages silken firm tofu

4 cups soymilk or rice milk

½ cup sucanat, or maple syrup

½ cup canola oil

Raspberries, strawberries, and/or blueberries, about a cup in all, or more if you like it super fruity

Blend all the ingredients well until frothy, and chill for 15 to 30 minutes. Serve with a cinnamon stick and enjoy!

Per serving: Calories 492, Protein 12 g,
Fat 33 g, Carbohydrates 11 g

Orange Dream

Makes 4 servings

½ cup frozen orange juice concentrate

2 cups nondairy milk

½ cup powdered soymilk

1 teaspoon pure vanilla extract

1 cup crushed ice

Blend all the ingredients well. Garnish with a slice of orange, and lick your lips when finished!

Per serving: Calories 154, Protein 12 g,
Fat 2 g, Carbohydrates 21 g

Variations

Pineapple, apple, or other juice concentrate will work well in place of the orange juice concentrate.

Add a little fresh pineapple.

Fresh fruit juice will work but will not have as strong a flavor as the juice concentrate. Fresh oranges will be too stringy in the blender.

Banana Cappuccino Froth

Makes 2 servings

Use either coffee or a grain beverage, depending on how wide awake you want to be after you drink this!

2 frozen bananas

1 cup nondairy yogurt

1 cup prepared coffee or grain beverage

2 tablespoons sugar or brown rice syrup

¼ cup crushed ice (optional)

Blend all the ingredients well, and serve in a tall, frosted glass after dinner, for summer brunch, or any time at all!

Per serving: Calories 192, Protein 4 g,
Fat 3 g, Carbohydrates 38 g

Ironman Shake

Makes 2 servings

This tastes somewhat like an oatmeal cookie, but it's packed with nutrition, especially iron and calcium from the molasses.

¼ cup pitted prunes, soaked in distilled water

¼ cup quick oats

2 tablespoons protein powder

2 tablespoons maple syrup

½ teaspoon blackstrap molasses (optional)

2 scoops nondairy yogurt or frozen dessert

1 cup nondairy milk

1 teaspoon pure vanilla

Blend all the ingredients well, and get ready to take on the world!

Per serving: Calories 245, Protein 12 g, Fat 3 g, Carbohydrates 42 g

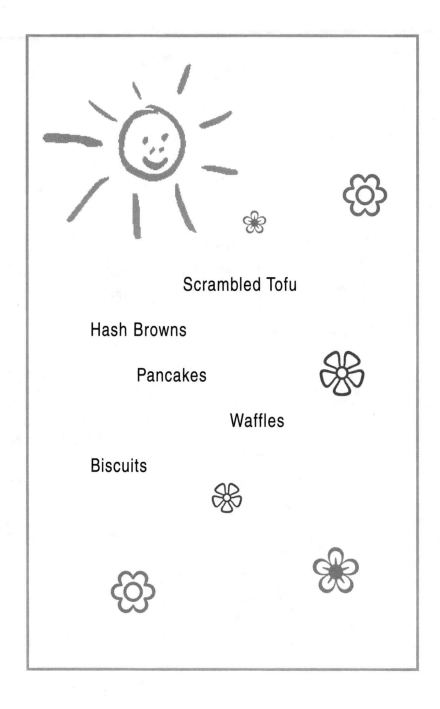

Scrambled Tofu

Hash Browns

Pancakes

Waffles

Biscuits

Muffins

Blueberry Muffins

Date Muffins

Breakfast in a Crockpot

SCRAMBLED TOFU

Makes 4 servings

Here's a quick and easy alternative to a popular egg dish. The turmeric, a delicately flavored spice, adds a nice yellow color.

1 pound medium or firm tofu, sliced and drained well between towels

¼ teaspoon garlic powder

¼ teaspoon turmeric

⅛ teaspoon pepper

Salt to taste

Place the tofu in a large bowl, and mash with a fork. Add the spices and mix well.

Heat a large nonstick skillet over medium heat. Place the tofu in the pan, and cook, stirring frequently, until hot.

Per serving: Calories 86, Protein 8 g, Fat 5 g, Carbohydrates 2 g

Variations

Cook some chopped onions and/or green pepper in the skillet in 1 or 2 teaspoons of oil until nicely browned before adding the tofu.

Makes 4 servings

These all-time favorites have a minimum amount of oil and a maximum amount of flavor. They're great as a side dish with dinner, or a perfect brunch dish alongside Scrambled Tofu, page 56.

1 tablespoon vegetable oil

4 cups cold, cooked potatoes, cut into ¼- to ½-inch cubes (If the potatoes have been baked, carefully remove the skins. If the potatoes have been boiled, the skin is usually soft enough to leave on.)

1 cup finely chopped onions

Salt, pepper, and paprika to taste

Heat the oil in a large nonstick skillet over medium heat. Add the potatoes and onions. Sprinkle with salt and pepper to taste and lots of paprika. Cook, stirring frequently, for about 10 minutes, or until the edges of the potatoes are brown and crisp.

Per serving: Calories 180, Protein 2 g, Fat 3 g, Carbohydrates 35 g

HASH BROWNS

Variations

Add ½ cup finely chopped green pepper along with the onions and potatoes.

PANCAKES

Makes 10 to 12 pancakes

You can tell the griddle is ready if a few drops of water sprinkled on it bounces. Some griddles need oil. Always make a test pancake first to see if the pan is hot enough.

1 cup unbleached white flour

1 cup whole wheat pastry flour

1 tablespoon baking powder

1 tablespoon sugar

2 tablespoons oil

2 cups soymilk or rice milk

Combine all the ingredients in a bowl and stir. The batter will be lumpy.

Heat a heavy griddle on medium high. Use a ⅓ cup measure to scoop out the batter for the test cake. It will be ready to turn over when bubbles appear on the top. If it browns too fast, lower the heat. Continue until all the batter is used up. Cover the pancakes with a clean dish towel to keep warm.

Per 3 pancakes: Calories 355, Protein 11 g, Fat 10 g, Carbohydrates 53 g

Variations

Why stop at plain pancakes when there are so many wonderful fruits you can add to the batter to make exotic, vitamin-rich breakfast specials. Blueberries, of course, are a classic, as well as bananas. Try applesauce or a dash of cinnamon. You can also add a little wheat germ, protein powder, or other nutritional supplement.

Makes about 6 waffles

Read the directions for the waffle iron you use. Most have an indicator light that turns off when the iron is hot enough to begin cooking. Oil the iron if needed. The waffle is done when the iron stops steaming. Don't open the lid to peek while it is cooking!

1 cup unbleached white flour

1 cup whole wheat pastry flour

1 tablespoon baking powder

½ teaspoon salt

¼ cup canola oil

1½ cups soymilk or rice milk

Egg replacer equal to 2 eggs

1 tablespoon sugar

½ to 1 cup chopped pecans (optional)

Sift the flour, baking powder, and salt into a medium bowl.

In a small bowl, beat together the oil, milk egg replacer, sugar, and pecans. Stir the liquid into the flour mixture, but do not overmix.

Use a cup to pour the batter onto the heated waffle iron. Make a test waffle first; then you will know how much batter to use. Bake until no steam comes out. The waffle should be golden brown.

Per waffle: Calories 255, Protein 8 g, Fat 11 g, Carbohydrates 31 g

Vegan Egg Alternative

Instead of 2 eggs, you can use 1 tablespoon Ener-G Egg replacer mixed with ¼ cup water, or 4 teaspoons flaxseeds blended with ¼ cup warm water in a blender until thickened.

BISCUITS

Makes twelve 3-inch biscuits

1 cup whole wheat flour
1 cup all-purpose flour
1 tablespoon baking powder
½ teaspoon salt
3 tablespoons vegetable oil
1 cup low-fat soymilk

Preheat the oven to 450°F.

Lightly oil a baking sheet, or spray with a nonstick cooking spray.

Into a large bowl, sift the flours, baking powder, and salt. Gently stir any bran that is left in the sifter back into the flour.

Add the oil. Mix with a fork or pastry blender until the mixture resembles coarse crumbs. Add the milk and stir until the dry ingredients are moistened.

Place the dough on a floured surface, and knead a few times until the dough holds together in a ball. (If the dough is sticky, you may need to add a bit more flour.) Place a sheet of wax paper over the dough and roll out to ½-inch thickness. Carefully remove the wax paper.

Using a 3-inch biscuit cutter or a glass, cut out 12 biscuits. (The scraps can be put together and rolled out again.)

Place the biscuits on the prepared baking sheet, and bake for 10 minutes until the bottoms of the biscuits are lightly browned.

Remove to a wire rack, and serve warm for best flavor. Leftovers can be reheated in a toaster or oven.

Per biscuit: Calories 105, Protein 3 g, Fat 3 g, Carbohydrates 15 g

Makes 12 muffins

The secret of light muffins is not overmixing the batter; try to combine the wet and dry ingredients with as few strokes as possible. The batter will be lumpy.

1 cup unbleached flour

1 cup whole wheat pastry flour

¼ cup sugar

2 teaspoons baking powder

½ teaspoon salt

Egg replacer for 1 egg (½ tablespoon Ener-G Egg replacer mixed with 2 tablespoons water, or 2 teaspoons flaxseeds mixed with 2 tablespoons warm water in a blender until thickened)

½ cup oil

¾ cup water

Coat 12 large muffin tins with oil, or use baking cup liners in the tins. Preheat the oven to 350°F.

Sift together the flour, sugar, baking powder, and salt into a medium bowl. With a large spoon, make a well in the center of the dry ingredients.

In a small bowl, whisk together the egg replacer, oil, and water. Pour the wet ingredients into the dry ingredients, and combine, stirring only 20 to 25 times with a large spoon. It's okay for the batter to be lumpy.

Spoon the mixture into the oiled muffin tins, filling each about ⅔ full. Set the timer for 20 to 25 minutes, and bake until lightly browned on the top. Run a knife around the edge of each muffin tin to loosen the muffins before lifting out to a serving plate.

Per muffin: Calories 164, Protein 3 g, Fat 9 g, Carbohydrates 18 g

BLUEBERRY OR DATE MUFFINS

Makes 12 blueberry muffins

Blackberries are very good in muffins too.

1 cup fresh blueberries

Pick over the blueberries, rinse, and dry on paper towels. Prepare the recipe for Muffins on page 61. Gently stir in the berries after mixing the wet and dry ingredients. Be careful not to overmix. Continue with the recipe.

Makes 12 date muffins

The natural sweetness of dates makes them a perfect addition to muffins.

½ cup chopped, pitted dates

Prepare the recipe for Muffins on page 61. Before adding the liquid to the dry ingredients, put the dates in the flour mixture. Stir the dates around in the flour to coat evenly. Then add the liquid ingredients, and continue with the muffin recipe.

Vegan Alternative for Muffins

Many baking recipes call for eggs. Here's a healthy replacement that still gives you great baked goods. Instead of 1 egg, you can use ½ tablespoon Ener-G Egg replacer mixed with 2 tablespoons water, or 2 teaspoons flaxseeds combined with 2 tablespoons warm water in a blender until thickened.

Makes 6 servings

Any combination of grains will work in this easy, make-ahead breakfast. It's hot and steamy and ready whenever you are. Just throw all the ingredients into the crockpot, turn it on low, and go to sleep. It'll be ready when you wake up. A crockpot is great for soups and stews, too.

Once you find the combination of grains you like, you can save money by getting them in bulk at your favorite health food store. If you compare the nutritional benefits of various grains, you can find those that not only taste the best to you, but are also best for your individual dietary needs.

1 cup grains, uncooked (Try a combination of brown rice, millet, bulgur, barley, cornmeal, and rolled oats. If you don't have all of these, a few will do.)

⅓ cup raisins or any chopped dried fruit

1 unpeeled apple, chopped

1 teaspoon ground cinnamon

3½ cups water

1 teaspoon vanilla extract

Combine all the ingredients in a crockpot. Mix well, cover, and cook 8 hours on the low setting. Stir before serving.

Serve hot, topped with brown sugar or drizzled with maple syrup.

Per serving: Calories 91, Protein 2 g, Fat 0 g, Carbohydrates 19 g

BREAKFAST IN A CROCKPOT

Salads,

Macaroni Salad

Tofu Salad

Potato Salad

Tempuna Salad

Summer Fruit Salad

Mexican Salad in a Burrito

Dressings,

Orange-Basil Vinaigrette

Tofu Dressing

Thousand Island Dressing

French Dressing

Yogurt Tahini Sauce

Celery Seed Salad Dressing

Miso Dressing

Herb Dressing

Spreads,

Olive Nut Spread

Peanut Butter Orange Spread

Hummus

Melty Cheeze Spread

Sweet and Sour Dipping Sauce

Maple Mustard Sauce

 # and Dips

Onion Soup Dip

Chili Yogurt Dip

Warm Chili con Queso Dip

Easy Guacamole

Black Bean and Corn Salsa

macaroni

Makes 8 servings

Other kinds of pasta besides macaroni can be used in this salad. Try small shells or spirals (rotelle). Follow directions on the package for cooking the pasta.

3 quarts water

2 cups elbow macaroni

2 tablespoons oil

2 tablespoons vinegar

3 green onions, chopped

1 cup finely chopped celery

2 carrots, grated

3 tablespoons soy mayonnaise

3 tablespoons soy sour cream

Heat the water in a large pot until boiling. Add the macaroni and boil for 8 to 10 minutes. Stir a few times with a wooden spoon so the macaroni doesn't stick to the bottom of the pan. Taste a piece to make sure it is tender. Drain the pasta in a colander.

Mix the oil and vinegar in a large serving bowl. Add the drained pasta and stir with a big spoon. Cover the bowl and chill the macaroni. When chilled, add the green onions, celery, and carrots.

Mix the macaroni with the vegetables, and add the mayonnaise and sour cream. You can also use only enough mayonnaise to moisten the noodles. Taste and add a little salt and a few dashes of pepper, if you like. Chill the salad until serving time.

Per serving: Calories 159, Protein 3 g,
Fat 5 g, Carbohydrates 23 g

tofu 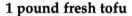 salad

Makes 4 servings

This is the vegetarian equivalent of egg salad.

1 pound fresh tofu
2 green onions, thinly sliced
2 stalks celery, finely chopped
1 medium carrot, grated
¼ cup soy mayonnaise
Chopped fresh herbs, or pickle relish
Nutritional yeast flakes (optional)
Chopped pickles (optional)
Salt and pepper

Drain the tofu in a colander. Using the large holes of the grater, grate the tofu or crumble it into a bowl.

Mix together the tofu and vegetables. Stir in the mayonnaise. You may want to add some fresh herbs, pickle relish, nutritional yeast flakes, or chopped pickles. Taste and add salt and pepper as needed.

Serve the salad on lettuce leaves, or use as a filling for sandwiches.

Per serving: Calories 141, Protein 9 g,
Fat 8 g, Carbohydrates 6 g

potato

Makes 6 servings

Start with this recipe and vary it to suit your particular tastes.

salad

2 quarts water

6 potatoes

¼ cup finely chopped onion

½ cup thinly sliced celery

1 carrot peeled and grated

¼ cup finely chopped fresh parsley

½ cup or more soy mayonnaise (just enough to moisten)

1 tablespoon wet mustard or 1 tablespoon pickle juice

Garnishes
Wedges of tomato
Slices of pickle
Sliced radishes

Heat the water in a large pot on medium-high.

Meanwhile, peel the potatoes or scrub them well, then cut them into quarters. Add them to the pot, set the timer for 20 to 30 minutes, and cook until they are tender. Drain the potatoes in a colander, and put into a bowl. Cover and cool before dicing.

Prepare the onion, celery, carrot, and parsley. Cut the cooled potatoes into smaller pieces, mix with the rest of the vegetables, and add the mayonnaise. Taste and add a little salt and pepper, if you like, along with the mustard or pickle juice.

Chill the salad. Before serving, decorate the top with one or more of the garnishes.

Per serving: Calories 174, Protein 2 g,
Fat 4 g, Carbohydrates 30 g

tempuna salad

Makes 6 servings

If you haven't eaten tempeh, this is a great way to try it out. Tempeh is a fermented soyfood made from soybeans or a mixture of soybeans and grains. Originally from Indonesia, tempeh has a mild, nutty flavor with a hint of mushrooms. It is usually found in the freezer section of natural food stores and Asian markets, and should be kept frozen after you get it home. Tempeh must be steamed for about 15 minutes before being eaten unless it is otherwise cooked. This recipe makes a delicious sandwich filling, especially topped with a slice of tomato.

8 ounces tempeh (defrosted if frozen)

1 small onion, chopped

2 stalks celery, chopped

2 tablespoons chopped fresh parsley

¼ cup chopped pickles

Enough soy mayonnaise to moisten

Put a steamer basket in a saucepan with a tightly fitting lid. Add water almost to the bottom of the basket. Heat to a simmer. Put the tempeh in the basket. Cover, set the timer for 15 minutes, and steam. Remove the tempeh from the pan, and cool.

Grate the tempeh into a medium bowl, using the large holes on the grater. Mix together the tempeh, vegetables, and mayonnaise. Taste the salad and add salt and pepper, if you like. Chill. Serve on lettuce or in sandwiches.

Per serving: Calories 118, Protein 6 g,
Fat 5 g, Carbohydrates 12 g

summer

Makes 6 servings

A fruit salad is always the number one favorite in hot weather. This can be served on lettuce as a first course, with or without Celery Seed Salad Dressing, page 75.

fruit salad

2 cups cubed watermelon

1 cup diced cantaloupe

**1 cup blueberries,
    washed and drained**

1 cup sliced strawberries

1 cup peeled, sliced peaches

1 apple, cut into small pieces

Prepare 5 or 6 cups of fresh fruit. You can use varying amounts of any fruits available. Mix the fruits together in a bowl, then chill.

Per serving: Calories 72, Protein 1 g,
Fat 0 g, Carbohydrates 16 g

mexican salad

Makes 2 servings

Any leftover salad will work. Ours is just a suggestion. Wrap your leftovers in a burrito, add salsa, and say, Olé!

in a burrito

2 flour tortillas

1 cup shredded romaine lettuce

½ cup chopped tomato

¼ cup chopped onion

2 tablespoons sliced black olives

½ cup shredded Cheddar-type soy cheese

1 teaspoon chili powder

Salsa or guacamole

Chopped jalapeño peppers, if desired

Preheat the oven to 350°F.

Wrap the tortillas tightly in aluminum foil and heat for 10 minutes.

While the tortillas are heating, combine the lettuce, tomato, onion, olives, and cheese in a small bowl. Sprinkle with the chili powder, and toss again.

Divide the mixture evenly onto the warm tortillas. Add salsa or guacamole and jalapeños if you are brave, and wrap the tortilla tightly around the filling. Serve right away.

Per serving: Calories 176, Protein 10 g,
Fat 7 g, Carbohydrates 20 g

Orange Basil Vinaigrette Salad Dressing

Makes 1¼ cups

This is a delicious alternative to bottled dressings.

¾ cup orange juice

¼ cup plus 2 tablespoons canola oil

4½ tablespoons red wine vinegar

1½ teaspoons dried basil

¼ teaspoon salt

¼ teaspoon pepper

⅛ teaspoon garlic powder

Combine all the ingredients in a bowl or jar, and mix well. Chill for several hours or overnight to blend flavors.

Per tablespoon: Calories 40, Protein 0 g, Fat 3 g, Carbohydrates 1 g

tofu dressing

Makes about 1⅓ cups

You can start with this basic recipe and add herbs, garlic, miso, nutritional yeast flakes, and other flavorings.

1 pound soft tofu, crumbled

¼ cup oil

2 tablespoons lemon juice

¼ teaspoon salt

Combine all the ingredients in a food processor or blender. Whip until smooth and creamy, scraping down the sides of the blender or processor when the motor is off.

Per tablespoon: Calories 40, Protein 2 g,
Fat 3 g, Carbohydrates 1 g

thousand island dressing

Makes 1 cup

This is also good as a sandwich spread.

1 cup soy mayonnaise

2 tablespoons chili sauce or ketchup

1 teaspoon grated onion

2 tablespoons finely chopped stuffed olives

Mix all the ingredients in a small bowl. Serve on lettuce, sliced tomatoes, or a salad of mixed greens.

Per tablespoon: Calories 38, Protein 0 g,
Fat 3 g, Carbohydrates 1 g

french dressing
Makes ½ cup

This is a classic dressing that's good to know how to make.

¼ cup vinegar
¼ teaspoon salt
6 tablespoons canola oil
1 teaspoon sugar
¼ teaspoon paprika

Put all the ingredients in a small jar, and shake well. Keep in a covered jar.

Per tablespoon: Calories 94, Protein 0 g,
Fat 10 g, Carbohydrates 1 g

yogurt tahini sauce
Makes about ¾ cup

This tart and creamy sauce also makes a great topping for baked potatoes or anything else that is normally topped with soy sour cream.

¼ cup tahini
2 tablespoons lemon juice
¼ teaspoon garlic powder
½ cup soy yogurt

Place the tahini in a small bowl. Add the lemon juice and garlic powder, and stir until well blended.

Add the yogurt, ¼ cup at a time, stirring until the mixture is smooth. Chili several hours to blend the flavors.

Per tablespoon: Calories 33, Protein 1 g,
Fat 2 g, Carbohydrates 2 g

celery seed salad dressing

Makes about 2 cups

This creamy dressing must be made in a blender or food processor. If you use a blender, be sure to stop the machine every minute or so and push the mixture down the sides with a rubber scraper.

1 cup crumbled tofu (½ pound)

½ cup canola oil

½ cup sugar

½ teaspoon salt

1 tablespoon celery seed

1 teaspoon wet yellow mustard

½ teaspoon paprika

Crumble the tofu into a blender or food processor. Add the rest of the ingredients, and pulse the blender or processor on and off, scraping down the sides, until the dressing is creamy and well mixed. Pour into a small pitcher for serving, and keep chilled.

Per tablespoon: Calories 47, Protein 0 g, Fat 3 g, Carbohydrates 3 g

miso dressing

Makes 1½ cups

Miso is a fermented soyfood that comes in a variety of flavors, colors, and concentrations. It is mostly salty, but can range from sweet to savory, with full-bodied flavors. A serving may be anywhere from a teaspoon to a tablespoon. Unpasteurized miso is a living food with friendly bacteria that can aid digestion. The beneficial enzymes in miso are destroyed by high heat, so don't boil it. The Japanese have been using miso for centuries. They attribute much of their good health to this tasty condiment.

¼ cup miso (It is available in different colors or strengths. Try a medium or dark colored miso for a richer flavor.)

¼ cup canola oil

¼ cup red wine vinegar

½ cup water

2 teaspoons liquid sweetener

2 teaspoons dried oregano

¼ teaspoon garlic powder

⅛ teaspoon pepper

Combine all the ingredients in a blender, and blend until smooth. Chill several hours to blend flavors. Keep refrigerated.

Per tablespoon: Calories 35, Protein 1 g,
Fat 3 g, Carbohydrates 1 g

herb dressing

Makes ¾ cup

Be creative. If you have fresh herbs, use them, but use twice as much. Any remaining dressing will keep for days in a covered jar.

¼ cup vinegar

½ teaspoon salt

¼ teaspoon dry mustard

¼ teaspoon pepper

½ cup olive oil

Dill weed

Basil

Oregano

Any herb or combination

In a small jar with a tight fitting lid, shake up the vinegar, salt, mustard, pepper, and oil. Add 1 teaspoon of one of the herbs for flavor.

Per tablespoon: Calories 81, Protein 0 g,
Fat 9 g, Carbohydrates 0 g

OLIVE NUT SPREAD

Makes almost 1 cup

½ cup chopped ripe olives or stuffed green olives
¼ cup chopped walnuts
2 tablespoons soy mayonnaise

Combine all the ingredients in a small bowl.

Per tablespoon: Calories 28, Protein 0 g,
Fat 2 g, Carbohydrates 1 g

PEANUT BUTTER ORANGE SPREAD

Makes about ⅓ cup

Almond butter also works in this delicious spread that tastes great on waffles, toast, or crackers.

¼ cup smooth or crunchy peanut butter
2 tablespoons frozen orange juice concentrate,
  thawed
⅛ teaspoon ground cinnamon
¼ teaspoon vanilla extract

In a small bowl, combine all the ingredients and mix well.

Per tablespoon: Calories 87, Protein 4 g,
Fat 6 g, Carbohydrates 5 g

HUMMUS

Makes 6 servings (⅓ cup per serving)

Chick-peas blended with lots of lemon and garlic make this creamy spread a sandwich-lover's delight. It's delicious piled into a pita pocket and topped with lettuce and tomatoes, or it can be used as a dip for fresh vegetables.

**1 (19-ounce) can chick-peas, rinsed and drained, or
  2 cups cooked chick-peas**

3 tablespoons lemon juice

¼ cup water

3 cloves garlic, crushed

¼ teaspoon salt

Dash of pepper

3 tablespoons tahini

1 tablespoon finely chopped fresh parsley

Paprika

In a blender, combine the chick-peas, lemon juice, water, garlic, salt, and pepper, and blend until smooth.

Spoon into a bowl and add the tahini, stirring until smooth. Sprinkle with the parsley and a light dusting of paprika. Cover and chill several hours or overnight to blend the flavors.

Per serving: Calories 135, Protein 5 g,
Fat 5 g, Carbohydrates 18 g

MELTY CHEEZE SAUCE

Makes 2½ cups

Nutritional yeast is delicious and easy to digest. Red Star Vegetarian Support Formula, also known as T-6635+, is a good source of vitamin B$_{12}$. It is available in both powder and flake form, and is often sold in bulk (measure out your own amount) in health food stores.

With a cheesy, nutty flavor and a golden color, you can use nutritional yeast with any number of foods. Try sprinkling some on your popcorn, or even on a bagel. Store it in a cool, dark place. Nutritional yeast flakes give a golden color and rich flavor to this dish.

½ cup nutritional yeast flakes

½ cup cornstarch

2 tablespoons flour

1 teaspoon salt

2 cups water

½ cup canola oil

1 teaspoon wet mustard

Mix the nutritional yeast, cornstarch, flour, and salt in a 1-quart saucepan. Whisk in the water, oil, and mustard. Cook and stir until the sauce thickens and bubbles. It will get thicker as it cools and can be thinned down with a little more water.

Per 2 tablespoons: Calories 73, Protein 1 g, Fat 5 g, Carbohydrates 118 g

SWEET AND SOUR DIPPING SAUCE

Makes about ⅓ cup

This sauce is great for dipping raw veggies as well as egg rolls.

¼ cup fruit-only peach or apricot jam

½ teaspoon dry mustard

1 teaspoon reduced-sodium or regular soy sauce

1 teaspoon white vinegar

1 teaspoon water

In a small bowl or custard cup, combine all the ingredients, mixing well. Add more water if a thinner sauce is desired.

Per tablespoon: Calories 17, Protein 0 g,
Fat 0 g, Carbohydrates 4 g

MAPLE MUSTARD SAUCE

Makes about ⅓ cup

This quick, easy sauce is also great on sandwiches.

¼ cup Dijon mustard

2 tablespoons maple syrup

Combine the mustard and maple syrup in a small bowl, and mix well.

Per tablespoon: Calories 39, Protein 0 g,
Fat 3 g, Carbohydrates 2 g

ONION SOUP DIP

Makes 2 cups

⅓ cup dried onion soup mix

2 cups soy sour cream

Stir together the soup mix and sour cream until well mixed.
Cover the bowl and chill 2 hours before serving.

Per 2 tablespoons: Calories 46, Protein 1 g,
Fat 3 g, Carbohydrates 5 g

CHILI YOGURT DIP

Makes about 2 cups

2 cups plain soy yogurt

2 tablespoons extra-virgin olive oil

2 green onions, chopped

1 teaspoon chili powder

¼ teaspoon black pepper

Blend all the ingredients together until smooth. Taste and
add a little salt if needed. Chill. Serve with raw veggies.

Per 2 tablespoons: Calories 25, Protein 1 g,
Fat 1 g, Carbohydrates 1 g

WARM CHILI CON QUESO DIP

Makes about 2 cups

This is great with corn chips or tortillas.

1 (8-ounce) jar picante or taco sauce
½ teaspoon garlic powder
1 cup grated soy Jack cheese (4 ounces)

Heat the sauce and garlic powder in a small pan. When it's warm, stir in the cheese to melt.

Per 2 tablespoons: Calories 21, Protein 2 g,
Fat 1 g, Carbohydrates 2 g

EASY GUACAMOLE

Makes 1 cup

1 medium, ripe avocado, peeled, pit removed
1 teaspoon lemon juice
1 tablespoon very finely chopped onion
½ cup finely chopped tomato
¼ teaspoon garlic powder
⅛ teaspoon chili powder
Dash of salt and pepper

Place the avocado in a bowl, and mash with a fork until smooth. Add the remaining ingredients and mix well. Serve right away or wrap tightly and chill.

Per 2 tablespoons: Calories 23, Protein 0 g,
Fat 1 g, Carbohydrates 2 g

BLACK BEAN AND CORN SALSA

Makes 4 cups (8 servings)

Scoop up this chunky salsa with tortilla chips for an irresistible appetizer or snack.

2 (15-ounce) cans chopped tomatoes, drained

1 (1-pound) can black beans, rinsed and drained

1 cup canned corn, drained

¼ cup chopped onion

½ cup chopped celery

1 (4-ounce) can chopped hot or mild green chiles, drained

1 tablespoon red wine vinegar

2 teaspoons liquid sweetener

1 teaspoon ground coriander

1 teaspoon ground cumin

¼ teaspoon garlic powder

¼ teaspoon salt

Pepper to taste or chopped jalapeños

In a medium bowl, combine all the ingredients, mixing well. Chill for several hours or overnight to blend flavors.

Stir before using. Serve cold with tortilla chips.

Per serving: Calories 62, Protein 3 g,
Fat 0 g, Carbohydrates 13 g

Soups

Lentil Soup

Vegetable Soup

Miso Soup with Tofu

Corn Chowder

Black Bean Soup

Minestrone

Lentil Soup

Makes 6 servings

Lentils are high in protein, making this a hearty, filling soup.

1 pound dry lentils

8 cups water

1 bay leaf

2 cloves garlic, finely chopped

2 celery stalks, finely chopped

1 large onion, finely chopped

¼ cup oil

¼ cup tomato sauce or catsup

1 teaspoon salt

¼ teaspoon pepper

Rinse the lentils well and drain in a colander. Place in a large pot with the water and bay leaf. Cover the pot and bring to a boil over high heat. Reduce the heat to low, and cook the lentils for 30 minutes.

Meanwhile, prepare the garlic, celery, and onion. Heat the oil in a frying pan over medium-low heat. Fry the onions and garlic in the oil for 10 minutes. Add the celery and cook 5 minutes more.

Add the cooked vegetables to the soup pot along with the tomato sauce, salt, and pepper. Cover the pot and cook over medium heat about 20 minutes more, stirring once in a while. Add more seasonings to taste, if you want. Remove the bay leaf before serving.

Per serving: Calories 187, Protein 6 g,
Fat 9 g, Carbohydrates 19 g

egetable Soup

Makes 8 servings

This is a great way to serve up vegetables, if you have a lot on hand.

1 large onion, peeled
½ head cabbage
3 carrots
4 stalks celery
¼ cup oil
2 quarts warm water
1 teaspoon salt
2 vegetable bouillon cubes, or 2 teaspoons
powdered vegetable bouillon

Slice or chop 2 quarts of fresh vegetables, such as onion, cabbage, carrots, celery, or other vegetables. Heat the oil in a large, heavy kettle on low heat.

Add the onions, stir, and cook a few minutes, then add the cabbage. Cook and stir these for 10 minutes. Add the carrots and celery, and cook 10 minutes more. Add the water, salt, and bouillon. Bring to a boil, cover the pan, lower the heat, and simmer for about 20 minutes.

Per serving: Calories 95, Protein 1 g,
Fat 7 g, Carbohydrates 7 g

Miso Soup With Tofu

Makes 8 servings

Miso (see page 76) tastes a lot like soy sauce, only it's a solid paste. It makes soups, sauces, gravies, and casseroles taste good, but it can be salty, so add a little at a time.

8 cups water

2 tablespoons miso

¼ cup warm water

½ pound tofu, cut into small cubes

3 green onions, finely chopped

Bring the 8 cups of water to a boil. Stir the miso in the ¼ cup warm water until dissolved. Stir the miso mixture into the soup. Don't boil the soup after adding the miso.

Place the tofu in the soup to warm before you ladle the soup into bowls to serve. Sprinkle some of the green onions on the top of each soup bowl.

Per serving: Calories 31, Protein 2 g,
Fat 1 g, Carbohydrates 2 g

Corn Chowder

Makes 6 servings

Using frozen corn makes this a simple and delicious soup.

2 tablespoons vegetable oil

2 small potatoes, chopped

1 medium onion, chopped

2 stalks celery, chopped

1 tablespoon powdered vegetable bouillon

4 cups hot water

2 cups fresh or frozen corn kernels

1 cup soymilk

Heat the oil in a 2-quart pan. Cook the potatoes, onion, and celery in the oil for 5 minutes, then add the bouillon and hot water. Cover the pan, reduce the heat to low, and cook for 20 minutes.

Add the corn and soymilk to the soup. Cover and cook 10 minutes more on low heat.

Per serving: Calories 151, Protein 3 g, Fat 5 g, Carbohydrates 22 g

Black Bean Soup

Makes 6 to 8 servings

This can be a meal in itself, with warm bread and a salad.

1 pound black beans
3 quarts water for soaking
3 quarts fresh water
1 bay leaf
¼ cup olive oil
1 large onion, chopped
1 green pepper, chopped
5 cloves garlic, chopped
2 teaspoons cumin
2 teaspoons oregano
1 teaspoon salt
2 tablespoons vinegar

Wash the black beans and pick out any stones or shriveled beans. Soak the beans overnight in 3 quarts water. Drain the beans and add 3 quarts fresh water and the bay leaf. Bring the beans to a boil over high heat. Reduce the heat to low, cover the pan, and cook for 1 to 2 hours until the beans are tender. To see if the beans are done, squeeze one between your fingers; it should be very soft.

Heat the oil in a heavy skillet. Fry the vegetables until soft. Add to the beans with the cumin, oregano, salt, and vinegar. Simmer together about 30 minutes. Remove the bay leaf and serve the soup over a scoop of brown rice. Top with chopped red onions, if you like.

Per serving: Calories 165, Protein 5 g,
Fat 8 g, Carbohydrates 18 g

inestrone

Makes 6 servings

This is a good way to use up leftover beans or pasta or small amounts of any leftover cooked vegetables. This hearty soup makes a good meal served with salad and Italian bread or rolls.

¼ cup olive oil

1 onion, chopped

2 carrots

2 stalks celery

3 cups water

2 cups chopped tomatoes, or 1 (15-ounce) can

1 teaspoon garlic powder

½ teaspoon salt

2 cups cooked or canned beans

2 cups cooked small pasta (such as macaroni or spaghetti pieces)

Soy Parmesan, for topping

Heat the oil in a heavy 4-quart pot. Cook the onion in the oil over low heat while you chop the carrots and celery. Add them to the pan, and cook for about 5 minutes.

Add the water, tomatoes, garlic, and salt. Cook about 10 minutes, then add the beans and pasta. Cover and cook about 20 minutes. Ladle the soup into bowls, and serve with a side dish of Parmesan for topping.

Per serving: Calories 244, Protein 7 g,
Fat 9 g, Carbohydrates 33 g

MAIN

Egg Rolls

Vegetable Lo Mein

Rice with Herbs

Red Beans & Rice

Tofu Nuggets

Tofu Pot Pie

Baked Tofu

Noodle Casserole

Tacos

Taco Salad

Bean Burritos

Tofu Fajitas

Tofu Burritos

Enchilada Casserole

Hot Nacho Snacks

Chili

Chili Dogs

Lasagne

Italian Bean & Cheese Pockets

Pizza with The Works

Mini Pizzas

Veggie Reuben

T.L.T.

Potato Knishes

Almost French Fries

Falafel

Basic Rolls

Sesame Seed Rolls

Breadsticks

DISHES

EGG ROLLS

Makes 8 egg rolls

Making these Oriental favorites is easier than you think!

2 teaspoons soy sauce

2 teaspoons water

2 teaspoons cornstarch

1 teaspoon vegetable oil

1 teaspoon sesame oil

1½ cups finely shredded cabbage

1½ cups finely shredded Chinese cabbage

½ cup shredded carrots

½ cup canned bamboo shoots, cut into matchstick-size pieces

2 green onions, thinly sliced

1 package egg roll wrappers (Many Oriental grocery stores carry ones that are made without eggs.)

1 teaspoon all-purpose flour

1 tablespoon water

In a small bowl, combine the soy sauce, water, and cornstarch. Set aside.

Heat both oils in a large nonstick skillet over medium heat. Add both types of cabbage, the carrots, bamboo shoots, and green onions. Cook, stirring, until the vegetables are tender,

about 3 minutes. Stir the soy sauce mixture, and drizzle over the cabbage mixture. Cook, stirring, for 1 minute. Remove the skillet from the heat.

To assemble, place 2 tablespoons of the vegetable mixture diagonally across one wrapper, keeping the remaining wrappers covered with a damp towel to prevent drying. Fold the bottom comer over the filling, then fold over the left and right comers. Roll up the egg roll to enclose the filling. (Most packages of wrappers have handy diagrams to demonstrate the rolling process.) Combine the flour and water in a small bowl or custard cup. With your finger, spread a little on the last comer to seal the edges. Wrap any remaining wrappers tightly and refrigerate or freeze them for later use.

Heat the skillet over medium heat. Oil it lightly or spray with a nonstick cooking spray. With your finger, "paint" a small amount of oil on each egg roll. Place the egg rolls in the skillet and cook until brown on all sides, turning frequently. (If you make egg rolls cylindrical, rather than flat, they will brown more evenly.)

Serve with Maple Mustard or Sweet and Sour Dipping Sauces, page 81.

Per serving: Calories 46, Protein 1 g,
Fat 1 g, Carbohydrates 6 g

VEGETABLE LO MEIN

Makes 4 servings

Add any other vegetables you'd like to this delicious stir-fried favorite.

1 (8-ounce) package Oriental soba noodles

1 tablespoon oil

3 tablespoons reduced-sodium or regular soy sauce

2 cloves garlic, crushed

1 cup onions, cut into thin slivers

½ cup carrots, cut into matchstick-size pieces

1½ cups sliced mushrooms

½ cup thinly sliced green onions (green part only)

1 cup snow pea pods, cut diagonally into 1-inch
pieces

Cook the noodles according to package directions. Drain.

Heat 2 teaspoons of the oil and 2 teaspoons of the soy sauce in a large nonstick skillet or wok over medium heat. Add the garlic, onions, and carrots. Cook while stirring for 3 minutes.

Add the mushrooms. Cook while stirring for 3 more minutes. Add the green onions, pea pods, cooked noodles, and the remaining oil and soy sauce. Cook while stirring for 3 minutes or until the vegetables and noodles are mixed well and heated through.

Per serving: Calories 284, Protein 9 g,
Fat 4 g, Carbohydrates 52 g

RICE WITH HERBS

Makes 6 servings

To add a golden color to this, add ½ teaspoon turmeric along with the herbs.

3 tablespoons vegetable oil

1 onion, chopped

1 cup uncooked brown rice, washed

2½ cups water

1 teaspoon salt

½ teaspoon basil

½ teaspoon oregano

½ teaspoon garlic powder

¼ teaspoon pepper

Heat the oil, onion, and rice in a heavy 2-quart pan over medium heat. Fry the onions and rice for about 10 minutes, stirring.

Add the rest of the ingredients, and bring to a boil over high heat. Reduce the heat to low, cover the pan, set the timer for 40 to 45 minutes, and cook until the liquid is absorbed. Turn off the heat and let the rice set on the burner for 10 minutes, covered, before serving.

Per serving: Calories 165, Protein 2 g,
Fat 7 g, Carbohydrates 23 g

Red Beans & Rice

Makes 8 servings

Beans and rice are a staple in many diets around the world from Asia to Africa to South America, partly because this particular food combination is such an excellent source of protein.

1½ cups brown rice

3 cups water

1 teaspoon salt

1 large onion, chopped

2 tablespoons canola oil

½ teaspoon salt

1 tablespoon chili powder

1 teaspoon cumin powder

¼ teaspoon garlic powder

2 (15-ounce) cans red kidney beans, drained

Cook the rice, water, and salt in a saucepan until tender, about 45 minutes.

Heat a skillet and fry the onion in the oil over low heat until soft. Add the rest of the ingredients, and stir to combine.

Mix the rice, onion, and beans, and cook until hot. Serve with salsa and top with soy sour cream.

Per serving: Calories 287, Protein 11 g,
Fat 5 g, Carbohydrates 51 g

TOFU NUGGETS

Makes 4 servings

Freezing the tofu makes these nuggets wonderfully chewy on the inside. The wheat germ crust makes them deliciously crisp on the outside. The dipping sauces add the finishing touch!

1 pound firm tofu, frozen, thawed, and cut into 1-inch cubes

½ cup wheat germ

¼ heaping teaspoon garlic powder

⅛ teaspoon pepper

Salt to taste

Preheat the oven to 375°F.

Lightly oil a baking sheet, or spray with a nonstick cooking spray. Place the tofu cubes between layers of toweling, and gently squeeze out any excess water.

In a shallow bowl, combine the wheat germ and spices, and mix well.

Fill a small bowl with water.

Dip each piece of tofu first into the water, then shake off the excess water, and roll in the wheat germ. Gently press the wheat germ onto the tofu with the back of a spoon. Place the nuggets on the baking sheet. Bake 25 to 30 minutes until crisp. Serve with your choice of Dipping Sauces, pages 81-82.

Per serving: Calories 141, Protein 12 g,
Fat 6 g, Carbohydrates 8 g

*To freeze tofu, you may want to drain it slightly, then wrap it tightly in plastic wrap and place it in the freezer until it is solid. Thaw frozen tofu thoroughly before using.

TOFU POT PIE

Makes 6 to 8 servings

Vegetables in a yummy gravy under a pastry crust, baked to a golden brown, makes a wonderful dinner. Thaw frozen tofu before you start, or use fresh tofu.

Filling
4 cups water

3 medium potatoes, peeled and cut into chunks

3 carrots, peeled and thinly sliced

Gravy
¼ cup oil

1 large onion, chopped

½ cup sliced celery

1 pound defrosted tofu

2 tablespoons soy sauce

⅓ cup flour

½ teaspoon garlic powder

½ teaspoon oregano

2 teaspoons powdered vegetable bouillon

½ teaspoon thyme

½ teaspoon pepper

Bring the water to a boil. Add the potatoes and cover. Set the timer for 10 minutes, and cook. Add the carrots to the potatoes, and cook until the potatoes are tender. Drain, saving the liquid to use in the gravy, and set aside.

Heat a heavy 4-quart pot, and add the oil and onion. Cook over low heat until soft. Add the celery to the onion, and cook a few minutes more.

Press the liquid from the tofu, and cut or tear it into bite-sized pieces. Sprinkle the tofu a with the soy sauce. Mix in well. Add to the pan and stir in the flour.

To make the gravy, measure the potato cooking liquid into a 1-quart measure, and add enough water to make 4 cups. Pour into the pan and stir well. Add the garlic, oregano, bouillon, thyme, and pepper as you cook and stir the gravy. Cook the gravy for 10 minutes, then add the potatoes and carrots. Taste the gravy and add more seasonings, if you like.

Pour the filling into a round 2-quart baking dish. The dish should be 9 or 10 inches wide.

Pastry Crust and Assembly

1 cup unbleached white flour

1 cup whole wheat pastry flour

½ teaspoon salt

¾ stick margarine, or ⅔ cup oil

2 to 3 tablespoons ice water

Preheat the oven to 400°F.

Using a pastry blender, mix the flour, salt, and margarine until it looks like crumbs. Work in the ice water with a fork to make a ball of dough.

On a lightly floured surface, pat and roll the dough into a circle 1 inch bigger all around than the top of your baking dish. Carefully fold the pastry in half, and then in half again, so you can lift the pastry up and lay it on top of the pie filling. Unfold it to cover the pie. Turn the edges under neatly, then go around the rim of the crust with the tines of a fork, pressing the edges down to seal. Make six 2-inch slashes in the crust with a knife to let the steam escape while baking.

Set the pie on a baking sheet as it may bubble over. Set the timer for 30 minutes, and bake until the top is lightly browned.

Per serving: Calories 415, Protein 10 g,
Fat 20 g, Carbohydrates 47 g

BAKED TOFU

Makes 3 to 4 servings

1 pound tofu

Marinade
1 cup water
1 teaspoon thyme
2 tablespoons soy sauce
1 teaspoon marjoram
1 tablespoon nutritional yeast flakes

Breading mix
½ cup flour
2 tablespoons nutritional yeast flakes
1 teaspoon salt
1 teaspoon paprika

Wrap the tofu in a towel to drain.

To make the marinade, mix the water, thyme, soy sauce, marjoram, and 1 tablespoon nutritional yeast in a shallow pan.

Cut the tofu into 12 slices. Put them in the marinade, and let soak for 10 minutes.

To make the breading mixture, combine the flour, 2 tablespoons nutritional yeast, salt, and paprika in a large mixing bowl. Preheat the oven to 350°F.

Dip the tofu slices into the breading, and lay them out on a large, oiled baking sheet. Set the timer for 10 minutes, and bake the tofu. Turn the slices over, reset the timer for 10 minutes again, and bake on the other side.

Per serving: Calories 214, Protein 17 g,
Fat 6 g, Carbohydrates 21 g

NOODLE CASSEROLE

Makes 8 servings

13 quarts water
1 pound medium flat noodles
1 stick margarine, melted
1 teaspoon garlic powder
4 green onions, chopped
¼ cup finely chopped parsley
1 pound firm tofu, crumbled
¼ cup soy Parmesan
½ cup soy sour cream
¼ teaspoon pepper

Bring the water to a boil over high heat in a large kettle. Add the noodles and stir a few times with a big wooden spoon until the water boils again. Set the timer for about 8 minutes, and continue to stir. Taste a noodle to be sure it is cooked. Pour the noodles into a colander to drain, and cover with a towel so they don't dry out.

While the noodles are cooking, mix the margarine, garlic powder, onions, parsley, and tofu in a large bowl.

Preheat the oven to 350°F. Oil a 3-quart casserole. Mix the cooked noodles into the bowl with the melted margarine. Stir well, then stir in the Parmesan, sour cream, and pepper.

When the noodles and sauce are well mixed, put them in the oiled casserole, and cover with foil. Set the timer for 25 minutes, and bake in the hot oven.

Per serving: Calories 240, Protein 8 g,
Fat 16 g, Carbohydrates 16 g

TACOS

Makes 12 tacos

For toppings try chopped tomatoes, lettuce, onions, black olives, shredded soy cheese, and lots of salsa.

Taco filling
1 cup water

½ cup bulgur (cracked wheat)

2 teaspoons vegetable oil

½ cup chopped onions

½ cup chopped green pepper

1 (8-ounce) can salt-free or regular tomato sauce

1 (1-pound) can kidney beans, rinsed and drained, or 2 cups cooked beans

2 teaspoons chili powder

1 teaspoon ground cumin

¼ teaspoon garlic powder

⅛ teaspoon cayenne pepper

12 taco shells

Bring the water to a boil in a small saucepan. Add the bulgur. Cover, reduce the heat to low, and simmer for 15 minutes until the water has been absorbed.

Preheat the oven to 350°F. While the bulgur is cooking, heat the oil in a large nonstick skillet over medium heat. Add the onions and green peppers. Cook until tender, about 5 minutes.

Add the tomato sauce, beans, spices, and cooked bulgur. Mix well, mashing the beans with a fork. Cover, reduce the heat to low, and cook for 5 minutes.

Wrap the taco shells in foil and, while the filling is cooking, heat the shells in the oven for 5 minutes.

To serve, fill the shells with the bean mixture, then add your choice of toppings.

Per taco: Calories 106, Protein 3 g,
Fat 3 g, Carbohydrates 18 g

105

TACO SALAD

Makes 6 servings

All of the taco ingredients, piled high, make a filling meal-in-one. Why spend money eating out when you can make this at home!

1 recipe Taco filling, page 104

12 taco shells, broken into bite-size pieces, or one 7-ounce bag of baked tortilla chips

4 cups shredded lettuce

2 cups chopped tomato

¾ cup chopped onions

¼ cup thinly sliced black or green olives

6 ounces low-fat soy cheese, shredded (1½ cups)

Jar of mild or hot salsa

Prepare the taco filling according to directions.

To serve, arrange the broken taco shells on 6 dinner plates. Divide the lettuce evenly and place on the shells. Then top with the hot taco filling, tomato, onions, olives, cheese, and salsa.

Note: The nutritional analysis for this recipe was based on a serving size of 2 tablespoons of salsa. To reduce the amount of sodium, use smaller portions of salsa. You can also use regular soy cheese if extra calories are not a problem for you.

Per serving: Calories 340, Protein 14 g,
Fat 5 g, Carbohydrates 57 g

BEAN BURRITOS

Makes 12 burritos

It's so easy to make a complete meal with burritos. You can also add cooked rice, chopped avocado, fried green pepper strips, shredded cabbage, and almost anything else that strikes your fancy.

12 flour tortillas

3 cups hot cooked pinto beans

1 red onion, chopped

2 cups chopped lettuce

2 tomatoes, diced

1 cup grated soy cheese

Salsa

Soy sour cream (optional)

Brown the tortillas lightly on an oiled griddle. Put a big spoonful of the beans on each tortilla. Let people help themselves to the toppings and roll their own burritos.

Per burrito: Calories 169, Protein 8 g,
Fat 3 g, Carbohydrates 28 g

TOFU FAJITAS

Makes 6 fajitas

*These juicy fajitas can be served either plain or topped with salsa.
Marinate the tofu and vegetables ahead of time, and prepare the fajitas
"in a flash" when you're ready.*

1 pound firm tofu, cut into matchstick-size pieces

1½ cups thinly sliced onions

1½ cups thinly sliced green pepper

1 (4-ounce) can chopped green chiles

½ cup orange juice

1 tablespoon olive oil

2 tablespoons vinegar

3 cloves garlic, finely chopped

1 teaspoon ground cumin

1 teaspoon ground coriander

1 teaspoon dried oregano

6 (6-inch) flour tortillas

Place the tofu, onions, and green pepper in a 9- x 13-inch
baking pan. Cover the pan and refrigerate 4 or 5 hours,
gently stirring the tofu mixture occasionally.

In a small bowl, combine the remaining ingredients, except
the tortillas, and mix well. Pour over the tofu mixture.

To cook the fajitas, wrap the tortillas tightly in aluminum
foil and heat in a 350°F oven for 10 minutes.

Heat a large nonstick skillet over medium-high heat. Drain
the tofu mixture (reserving the marinade), and place in the
skillet. Cook, stirring gently, until the vegetables are slightly tender. Add the marinade a little at a time to keep the
mixture from sticking. (If you prefer a juicy fajita filling,
add all of the marinade.)

To serve, spoon the tofu filling into the center of the heated tortillas, roll, and enjoy.

Per serving: Calories 199, Protein 8 g,
Fat 8 g, Carbohydrates 25 g

Makes 12 burritos

Use firm or extra-firm tofu for these, so your filling won't drip out the end of your burrito.

1 teaspoon flour

2 teaspoons chili powder

1 teaspoon cumin

1 teaspoon salt

½ teaspoon basil or oregano

1 pound tofu

3 tablespoons oil

12 flour tortillas

Mix the flour, chili powder, cumin, salt, and basil in a medium bowl. When spices are mixed, crumble in the tofu and mix.

Heat a heavy skillet on medium heat, and add the oil and seasoned tofu mix. Fry for about 5 minutes, using a spatula to keep it from sticking to the pan as it heats.

Put the tofu mixture into tortillas, and prepare and serve accompaniments as for Bean Burritos, page 107.

Per serving: Calories 139, Protein 5 g,
Fat 7 g, Carbohydrates 15 g

Enchilada Casserole

Makes 8 servings

A big pan of enchiladas is always a hit and well worth the time it takes to make. Leftovers are great for lunch or a snack. Enchiladas are also good with the filling for Tofu Burritos, page 109.

Chili Gravy (6 cups)

⅓ cup vegetable oil

2 onions, chopped

½ cup flour

2 tablespoons chili powder

1 tablespoon cumin powder

1 teaspoon garlic powder

1 teaspoon salt

¼ teaspoon pepper

6 cups warm water

12 flour tortillas

4 cups cooked pinto beans

2 cups Melty Cheeze Sauce, page 80,
   or grated soy cheese

To make the gravy, heat the oil in a heavy 3- or 4-quart pot over low heat, add the onions, and fry until soft. Sprinkle the flour, chili powder, cumin, garlic powder, salt, and pepper onto the onions, and stir. Slowly add the water to the pot. Keep stirring with a whisk to work out the lumps as you add the water. Cook this gravy over low heat for 20 minutes, whisking sometimes so it doesn't stick or get lumpy.

Preheat the oven to 350°F.

To assemble the enchiladas, spread 2 cups of the chili gravy over the bottom of an oiled 9- x 13-inch pan.

Heat a heavy skillet or griddle, oil it lightly, and cook the tortillas on each side for about 30 seconds. Spread a big spoonful of beans down the middle of each tortilla, roll it up, set it in the gravy in the pan. Continue to cook, fill, and roll until all the tortillas and beans are used. Pour the remaining gravy over the enchiladas. Top the casserole with the soy cheese or cheeze sauce.

Set the timer for 40 minutes, and bake the casserole in the hot oven. Cut into squares to serve.

Per serving: Calories 510, Protein 13 g,
Fat 22 g, Carbohydrates 61 g

HOT NACHO SNACKS

Makes 8 servings

This crunchy "finger-food" treat is great for snacks or parties.

1 large (7-ounce) bag baked tortilla chips

6 ounces shredded low-fat soy cheese (1½ cups)

1 large tomato, chopped into ½-inch pieces

¼ cup thinly sliced black olives or a combination of black olives and stuffed green olives

2 tablespoons thinly sliced green onions

1 cup shredded lettuce

Jar of mild or hot salsa

Preheat the oven to 375°F.

Spread the tortilla chips evenly in an ungreased 10- x 15-inch shallow baking pan. Sprinkle with half of the cheese, followed by the tomato, olives, green onions, and then the remaining cheese. Bake until the cheese is melted, about 5 minutes.

Remove from the oven and top with lettuce. Serve with salsa on the side.

Per serving: Calories 97, Protein 4 g,
Fat 2 g, Carbohydrates 14 g

CHILI SIN CARNE

Makes 6 servings

Chili is a vegetarian favorite. If you use textured soy protein granules, your family might not realize they're not eating meat.

1 cup textured soy protein granules

⅞ cup boiling water

1 medium onion, finely chopped

1 clove garlic, finely chopped

2 tablespoons vegetable oil

1 (16-ounce) can diced tomatoes (2 cups)

2 cups water

2 tablespoons chili powder

1 teaspoon cumin powder

1 teaspoon salt

2 cups cooked pinto or red kidney beans (with their liquid, if canned)

Measure the textured soy protein granules and ⅞ cup water into a small bowl and stir.

In a heavy 2-quart pan, fry the onion and garlic in the oil over low heat until the onions are soft. Add the reconstituted granules, and fry for 5 minutes.

Add the tomatoes, 2 cups water, chili powder, cumin, and salt. Bring to a boil, reduce the heat, cover, and cook on low for 20 minutes. Break up the tomatoes if they are still in big pieces, then add the beans. Cook for 20 minutes. Taste and add more seasonings, if you like.

Per serving: Calories 184, Protein 12 g,
Fat 4 g, Carbohydrates 23 g

CHILI DOGS

Makes 12 "dogs"

Dough
1 tablespoon baking yeast
¼ cup warm water
1 teaspoon sugar
¾ cup warm water
2 cups flour
2 tablespoons oil
1 cup flour
½ teaspoon salt

Chili Filling
1 cup textured soy protein granules
⅞ cup boiling water
2 tablespoons oil
1 medium onion, finely chopped
1 clove garlic, finely chopped
1 (6-ounce) can tomato paste plus 1 can water
1 teaspoon cumin
½ teaspoon garlic powder
½ teaspoon salt
1 teaspoon chili powder
½ teaspoon oregano

In a large bowl, combine the yeast, ¼ cup warm water, and sweetener, and gently stir until the yeast is dissolved. Add the ¾ cup warm water, 2 cups flour, and oil. Beat 100 times, then let it rest for 10 minutes. Beat in 1 cup flour and the salt. If the dough is sticking, add a little more flour. Pat some oil on top of the dough, cover the bowl, and let the dough rise in a warm place for 1 hour.

Mix the textured soy protein granules and boiling water together in a 2-quart bowl.

Heat the oil in a heavy 2-quart saucepan, and add the onion and garlic. Fry the onions and garlic for 5 minutes over medium heat, then add the reconstituted granules, and cook 5 minutes more. Add the tomato paste, cumin, garlic powder, salt, chili powder, and oregano. Cook and stir this mixture for 10 minutes.

Lightly oil 2 cookie sheets. With oily fingers, press down the dough, and divide into 2 balls. Sprinkle flour on a board and a rolling pin. Lightly roll out 1 ball of dough into a rectangle about 12 inches long.

Spread half of the filling mixture on the dough, then roll it the long way. Slice into 6 pieces, and put each slice on the baking sheet. Oil the tops. Repeat with the remaining dough and filling.

Preheat the oven to 350°F. Meanwhile, let the chili dogs rise for 10 or 15 minutes on the baking sheet. Set the timer for 25 to 30 minutes, and bake until lightly browned.

Per serving: Calories 182, Protein 7 g,
Fat 5 g, Carbohydrates 27 g

LASAGNE

Makes 6 servings

You'll be pleased to find that this favorite dish is not hard to make. No need to cook the noodles first, just layer them right out of the package.

1 (32-ounce) jar pasta sauce

½ pound lasagne noodles (9 large noodles)

1 pound tofu, well-drained and crumbled

2 cups Melty Cheeze Sauce, page 80, or ½ pound soy mozzarella, grated

Preheat the oven to 350°F.

Spread a little of the pasta sauce on the bottom of an oiled 9- x 13-inch pan that is at least 2 inches deep. Layer half the noodles on the sauce. Dot the noodles with spoonfuls of the tofu. Sprinkle on half the cheeze sauce or grated cheese. Spread with half of the remaining pasta sauce.

Make another layer of noodles, then the rest of the tofu, then the rest of the pasta sauce, and top with the last of the cheeze sauce. Cover the pan with aluminum foil.

Set the timer for 45 minutes, and bake in the hot oven. Remove the foil, reset the timer for 15 minutes, and continue to bake. Cool for 5 or 10 minutes before cutting into squares to serve.

Per serving: Calories 476, Protein 16 g, Fat 19 g, Carbohydrates 56 g

To make this recipe into a more well-rounded meal, try adding some thinly sliced vegetables such as zucchini, mushrooms, spinach, peppers, and/or onions. You can also spice up the tofu with garlic powder, lemon juice, or other seasonings before layering it in the casserole.

ITALIAN BEAN AND CHEESE POCKETS

Makes 2 servings

A great meal or snack. Feel free to add chopped jalapeños, if you dare.

2 small pita bread pockets

½ cup canned kidney beans or pinto beans, rinsed and drained

2 tablespoons finely chopped onion

½ cup chopped tomato

½ cup shredded mozzarella-type soy cheese

2 tablespoons chopped black olives

1 tablespoon Italian dressing

Preheat the oven to 400°F.

Split open one end of each pita bread pocket.

In a large bowl, combine the remaining ingredients. Divide the filling evenly and spoon into the open end of each pita pocket. Wrap each sandwich tightly in a piece of aluminum foil, and bake for 20 minutes. Serve hot.

Per serving: Calories 300, Protein 13 g, Fat 8 g, Carbohydrates 43 g

PIZZA WITH THE WORKS

Makes 4 servings

You can make this easy pizza at home in less time than it takes to run out and buy one. If you prefer, leave off the cheese and pile on more veggies, or serve with a salad for a well-balanced meal.

Crust

¾ cup whole wheat flour

¾ cup all-purpose flour

1 teaspoon baking powder

¼ teaspoon salt

¾ cup plus 1 tablespoon water

Sauce

1 (8-ounce) can tomato sauce

¼ teaspoon dried oregano

¼ teaspoon dried basil

⅛ teaspoon garlic powder

Topping

6 ounces low-fat soy cheese, shredded (1½ cups)

¼ cup chopped or thinly sliced onions

1 cup coarsely chopped mushrooms

½ cup chopped green pepper

¼ cup sliced pitted black olives

Preheat the oven to 400°F. Lightly oil a 12-inch pizza pan, or spray with nonstick cooking spray. In a large bowl, combine both types of flour, baking powder, and salt. Mix well. Add the water, mixing until all the ingredients are moistened. With your hands, work the dough into a ball. Place the dough on the prepared pan. Press into the pan to form a crust, flouring your hands slightly to avoid sticking. Bake for 10 minutes. Remove the pan from the oven.

Combine the tomato sauce and spices, mixing well. Spread evenly over the baked crust, staying ½ inch away from the edge of the pan. Evenly sprinkle on the cheese and then the vegetables over the sauce. Bake for 10 to 15 minutes until the cheese is melted.

Per serving: Calories 232, Protein 11 g,
Fat 2 g, Carbohydrates 40 g

MINI PIZZAS

Makes 12 servings

This is a quick and easy way to get a pizza treat.

1 (8-ounce) can tomato sauce

1 teaspoon oregano

1 teaspoon basil

6 English muffins, cut in half

1 onion, thinly sliced

1 green pepper, thinly sliced

½ cup sliced stuffed olives

1 cup grated soy cheese (4 ounces)

Mix the tomato sauce, oregano, and basil in a small bowl. Spread the English muffins with the tomato mixture, then arrange the onions, peppers, olives, and cheese on top.

Heat the broiler and place the muffin halves on a cookie sheet. Put under the broiler on an oven rack about 4 inches from the heat, leaving the oven door open. Broil until the cheese bubbles. Serve hot.

Per serving: Calories 109, Protein 5 g,
Fat 2 g, Carbohydrates 17 g

VEGGIE REUBEN

Makes 2 sandwiches

This veggie version of a popular deli sandwich is chock full of delicious vegetables and flavors.

1½ cups finely shredded cabbage

⅓ cup very thinly sliced onions

⅓ cup sweet red pepper, cut into matchstick-size pieces

1 tablespoon lemon juice

4 slices rye bread

2 ounces soy cheese, sliced or shredded (½ cup shredded)

Dressing

2 teaspoons soy mayonnaise

2 teaspoons ketchup

1 teaspoon sweet pickle relish

Pinch of garlic powder

Pinch of pepper

Lightly oil a large, nonstick skillet, or spray with nonstick cooking spray. Heat over medium heat. Add the cabbage, onions, red pepper, and lemon juice. Cook, stirring, until the vegetables are tender, about 5 minutes. Add small amounts of water, if necessary to prevent sticking.

Divide the mixture evenly and pile onto 2 slices of the bread. Divide the cheese and place over the vegetables.

Combine the dressing ingredients in a small bowl. Spread the dressing on the remaining bread slices; assemble the sandwiches.

Reheat the skillet over medium heat. Again, oil it lightly or spray with nonstick cooking spray. Place the sandwiches in the skillet and cook, turning several times, until both sides are toasted and the filling is hot.

Per sandwich: Calories 271, Protein 14 g,
Fat 6 g, Carbohydrates 38 g

T. L. T.

Makes 2 sandwiches

This sandwich is quick, easy, and super-delicious. Filled with crisp slices of tofu, it makes a great last minute lunch or dinner.

6 ounces firm tofu, sliced ⅛ inch thick

2 teaspoons soy sauce

4 slices whole wheat bread, toasted

4 lettuce leaves

2 slices of tomato

2 tablespoons soy mayonnaise

Heat a nonstick skillet or griddle over medium heat. Lightly drizzle the soy sauce over the tofu slices, using about ⅛ teaspoon on each slice. Place the tofu in a skillet. Cook, turning several times, until the tofu is crisp.

Place the tofu on the toast with the lettuce, tomato, and mayonnaise.

Per sandwich: Calories 211, Protein 11 g,
Fat 9 g, Carbohydrates 17 g

POTATO KNISHES

Makes 4 knishes

Bite into one of these potato patties and taste the surprise onion filling. It's a delicious recipe that can easily be doubled or tripled. The knishes freeze well and can be reheated in a toaster oven or microwave. For a full meal, add a salad, baked tofu, and rolls.

2 cups cooked potatoes, mashed (1½ pounds of potatoes, either baked or boiled, skins removed, will yield about 2 cups of mashed potatoes)

⅓ cup low-fat soymilk

1 tablespoon plus 1 teaspoon vegetable oil

1 tablespoon dried parsley flakes

Salt and pepper to taste (The knishes are best with lots of pepper.)

1 cup chopped onions

In a large bowl, combine the mashed potatoes, soymilk, 1 tablespoon of the oil, parsley, salt, and pepper. Mash well with a fork or potato masher. Add more milk, 1 teaspoon at a time, if the potatoes are too dry to hold together.

Heat the remaining 1 teaspoon of oil in a large nonstick skillet over medium heat. Add the onions and cook, stirring frequently, for 5 to 10 minutes until the onions are tender and nicely browned. Remove from the heat.

Divide the potato mixture evenly into 8 portions, and form each one into a 3-inch patty.

Divide the onions evenly and place in the center of 4 of the patties. Then top with remaining patties, making 4 thick knishes with the onions sandwiched in the middle. Press the edges together to seal.

Reheat the skillet over medium heat. Oil it lightly or spray with nonstick cooking spray. Place the knishes in the skillet and cook, turning several times, until nicely browned on both sides.

Per knish: Calories 129, Protein 2 g,
Fat 5 g, Carbohydrates 20 g

ALMOST FRENCH FRIES

Makes 4 servings

French fries without frying? Try them and you'll be amazed at how delicious they can be without any fat at all!

4 medium unpeeled baking potatoes, cut into strips

Salt and pepper to taste

Preheat the oven to 450°F.

Lightly oil a large baking sheet or spray with nonstick cooking spray. Arrange the potatoes on the prepared sheet in a single layer. Sprinkle with salt and pepper to taste.

Bake for 20 to 30 minutes, turning the potatoes several times, until the desired crispness is reached.

Per serving: Calories 145, Protein 2 g,
Fat 0 g, Carbohydrates 34 g

How to slice potatoes for fries:

If you watch late night tv or a home shopping channel, you may already have one of those unbelievable gadgets that lets you shove in a whole potato and it will automatically give you "perfect french fries every time." If not, here's one way to cut your potatoes.

Slice the potato in half lengthwise. Put each half down on the flat side, and slice lengthwise again, then continue slicing in the same way until that half is finished. When you spread the pieces out, you may have to cut some of them in half again to get them the desired size. Your fries won't be perfect according to some machine, but they'll be perfectly the size you want.

FALAFEL

Makes 5 servings (4 patties per serving)

Usually deep-fried, these spicy little chick-pea patties are browned in a nonstick pan, then piled into a pita bread and topped with lettuce, tomato, and a dollop of creamy Yogurt Tahini Sauce, page 74.

19-ounce can chick-peas, rinsed and drained, or 2 cups cooked chick-peas

2 tablespoons whole wheat flour

1 tablespoon vegetable oil

½ teaspoon garlic powder

½ teaspoon ground cumin

½ teaspoon ground coriander

⅛ teaspoon cayenne pepper

⅛ teaspoon salt

Place the chick-peas in a large bowl, and mash with a fork or potato masher. Add the flour and oil, and mix well. Sprinkle the spices evenly over the chick-peas, and mix well.

Form the mixture into balls, about 1¼ inches in diameter, then flatten the balls slightly to form patties. (If the mixture is a little dry, add water, 1 teaspoon at a time, until moist enough to hold together.)

Preheat a nonstick griddle or skillet over medium heat. Oil it lightly or spray with nonstick cooking spray. Place the patties on the griddle, and cook until brown and crisp, turning the patties several times and adding a little more cooking spray as needed.

Pile into pita breads while still hot. Add lettuce and tomatoes, or your choice of toppings, and a dollop of Yogurt Tahini Sauce, page 74.

Per serving: Calories 141, Protein 5 g,
Fat 4 g, Carbohydrates 20 g

BASIC ROLLS

Makes 16 rolls

1 tablespoon dry yeast

¼ cup warm water

1 tablespoon sugar

2 tablespoons oil

1 cup warm water

1 teaspoon salt

3½ to 4 cups flour

Mix the yeast, 1 tablespoon warm water, and sugar in a large bowl. Let the yeast dissolve, then stir in the oil and water. Stir in the salt and flour. Knead well. If the dough is sticky, add a little more flour.

Pat a little oil on the dough, cover the bowl with a towel, and let the dough rise in a warm place until it is double in size. This takes about 1 hour.

Oil a baking sheet. With oil on your fingers, press down the dough and divide it into 4 smaller balls. From each ball, shape 4 round rolls, and put them on the baking sheet. With your fingertip, lightly oil the tops of the rolls. Let them rise in a warm place for 10 minutes while the oven is heating.

Preheat the oven to 400°F. When the oven is hot, set the timer for 30 minutes, and bake the rolls until they are lightly browned on top.

Per serving: Calories 113, Protein 3 g,
Fat 2 g, Carbohydrates 21 g

SESAME SEED ROLLS

Makes 16 rolls

2 tablespoons sesame seeds, caraway seeds, or flaxseeds

Prepare the recipe for Basic Rolls from page 126. Before you put the rolls in the oven, place the sesame seeds in a saucer. As you shape each roll, dip the top into whatever seeds you are using. Bake as directed.

BREADSTICKS

Makes 20 breadsticks

Breadsticks are delicious with caraway or sesame seeds on top. Brush the sticks with oil before you sprinkle on the seeds, so the seeds will stay on while baking.

Prepare the recipe for Basic Rolls from page 126, and let the dough rise for 1 hour as directed. Pinch off a small ball of dough, and roll it between your hands into a stick about 6 inches long and ½ inch thick. Place the sticks on an oiled baking sheet.

Oil the tops of the sticks, and sprinkle with your choice of seeds. Let them rise for 10 minutes while the oven preheats to 400°F.

Bake for 10 minutes, then reduce the heat to 350°F, and bake for 10 minutes more. Watch carefully so the sticks don't burn.

Chocolate Tofu Cream Pie

Cheesecake

Blueberry Tofu Cheesecake

Pumpkin Pie

Chocolate Chip Bars

Carob Chip Brownies

Lemon Squares

Cinnamon Buns

Coffee Cake

Candy

Banana Nut Bread

Apple Cake

Apple Crisp

Fruit and Nut Candy Balls

Pudding

Banana Pudding

Super-Quick Rice Pudding

Nut Carob-Fudge Sundae

Tofu Whipped Topping

Lemon Frosting

Chocolate Frosting

ChoCOLaTe ToFu CreaM Pie

Here's an easy-to-make pie that's always a hit. There's no baking, just blend and cool.

Makes 8 servings

1½ pounds tofu, mashed

¾ to 1 cup sugar

3 to 4 tablespoons cocoa

Pinch of salt

1 tablespoon vanilla

1 (9-inch) graham cracker crust

Mix the tofu, sugar, cocoa, salt, and vanilla in a large bowl with a potato masher. Slowly add the mixture, ½ cup at time, to a blender. Blend each addition until smooth. Stop the blender, scrape down the sides, and stir as necessary.

When it is totally smooth and creamy, pour the filling into the pie crust, and refrigerate until firm.

Per serving: Calories 292, Protein 8 g, Fat 12 g, Carbohydrates 36 g

Variation

Add 2 tablespoons raspberry all-fruit jam for a little zing.

Who doesn't like cheesecake? This version is made like a pie, so you won't need any of the special pans used to make deli cheesecake.

Makes 8 servings

1 Graham Cracker Crust, page 132

1 pound tofu, crumbled

⅓ cup sugar

⅓ cup packed brown sugar

2 tablespoons lemon juice

¼ cup canola oil

2 tablespoons flour

1 teaspoon vanilla

¼ teaspoon salt

Don't pre-bake the crust for this cheesecake. Preheat the oven to 350°F.

Mix the tofu, sugar, brown sugar, lemon juice, and oil until smooth and creamy in a food processor. Or measure into a bowl and then mix in two batches in a blender. When the mixture is smooth, add the flour, vanilla, and salt.

Process until well mixed. If you have made it in 2 batches, stir them together. Pour the filling into the crust. Set the timer for 50 minutes, and bake. It's alright if small cracks appear in the top of the filling.

Per serving: Calories 239, Protein 5 g,
Fat 13 g, Carbohydrates 26 g

BlUeBerry ToFu CheeSeCaKe

Makes 16 servings

Graham Cracker Crust

¾ cup graham cracker crumbs

2 tablespoons nonhydrogenated margarine, melted

1 tablespoon maple syrup

Filling

2 pounds soft tofu

1 tablespoon lemon juice

3 tablespoons vegetable oil

½ cup low-fat soymilk

1⅓ cups sugar

1 tablespoon all-purpose flour

1 tablespoon plus 1 teaspoon vanilla extract

⅛ teaspoon lemon extract

⅛ teaspoon almond extract

Topping

2 cups fresh or frozen blueberries (If using frozen berries, there is no need to thaw them.)

2 tablespoons sugar

1 tablespoon plus 1 teaspoon cornstarch

⅔ cup water

Preheat the oven to 350°F.

Have a 9-inch springform pan ready. In the bottom of the pan, combine the graham cracker crumbs, margarine, and maple syrup. Mix well until the crumbs are moistened. Press the crumbs firmly into the bottom of the pan and about ½ inch up the sides. Bake for 8 minutes.

Slice the tofu into 1-inch slices, and place between layers of toweling. Gently squeeze out any excess water. Place half of the tofu in a blender with the lemon juice, vegetable oil, half of the milk, and half of the sugar. Blend until smooth. Spoon into a large bowl. Place the remaining tofu in the blender with the remaining milk, sugar, and other ingredients. Blend until smooth and add to the first mixture. Mix well. Pour into the prepared crust. Bake for 40 minutes or until set.

Place the blueberries and the 2 tablespoons sugar in a small saucepan. Dissolve the cornstarch in the water, and add to the saucepan. Cook over medium heat, stirring frequently, until the mixture comes to a boil. Continue to cook, stirring constantly, for 1 minute. Remove from the heat and let cool 10 minutes, then spoon over the cheesecake. Chill thoroughly.

Per serving: Calories 186, Protein 5 g,
Fat 7 g, Carbohydrates 26 g

Strawberry Cheesecake

Wash and slice 2 cups fresh strawberries. (Can be sweetened with a little sugar.) Arrange on top of the cooled cheesecake.

Chocolate or Carob Chip Cheesecake

As soon as the cheesecake comes out of the oven, dot the top with ½ cup chocolate or carob chips.

133

PuMpkIn PiE

This is best made with a food processor or blender to get a smooth, creamy consistency.

Makes 8 servings

1 recipe Pastry Crust, page 101

¾ pound tofu, crumbled

⅓ cup vegetable oil

1 teaspoon salt

1 cup (packed) brown sugar

3 tablespoons flour

1 (15-ounce) can pumpkin

1½ teaspoons cinnamon

¾ teaspoon powdered ginger

½ teaspoon nutmeg

2 teaspoons vanilla extract

Make the pastry crust on page 101, and have it ready in a pie pan. Preheat the oven to 400°F.

Put the tofu, oil, and salt in a food processor or blender, and process until smooth.

Blend the brown sugar, flour, pumpkin, cinnamon, ginger, nutmeg, and vanilla all at once in the processor, or measure into a bowl and process in 2 batches in a blender.

When the filling is well blended, pour it into the pastry shell. Set the timer for 10 minutes, and bake. Reduce the heat to 350°F, reset the timer for 40 to 45 minutes, and continue baking. Serve warm or chilled.

Per serving: Calories 410, Protein 7 g, Fat 22 g, Carbohydrates 44 g

Chocolate chip bars are even quicker to make than cookies.

ChoCoLatE ChiP BaRs

Makes 18 bars

1½ sticks nonhydrogenated margarine, softened

⅔ cup sugar

Egg replacer equal to 1 egg (½ tablespoon Ener-G
   Egg Replacer mixed with 2 tablespoons water, or
   2 teaspoons flaxseeds blended with 2
   tablespoons warm water until thickened)

¼ cup water

2½ cups flour

1½ teaspoons baking powder

¼ teaspoon salt

1 teaspoon vanilla

8 ounces chocolate or carob chips

Oil a 9- x 11 -inch pan. Preheat the oven to 350°F.

Cream together the margarine and sugar with a slotted spoon in a 2-quart bowl. When the mixture is creamy, stir in the egg replacer.

Sift the flour, baking powder, and salt onto a piece of waxed paper. Stir the flour mixture into the margarine and sugar until it is well mixed. The dough will be stiff. Stir in the vanilla and chocolate chips. Spread the dough evenly into the oiled pan.

Set the timer for 25 minutes, and bake until golden brown on top. Remove to a board and cool, but cut into 18 bars while still warm.

Per serving: Calories 214, Protein 2 g,
Fat 11 g, Carbohydrates 25 g

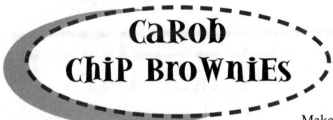

CaRob ChiP BroWniEs

Makes 16 brownies

1½ cups whole wheat flour

⅓ cup carob powder

1 teaspoon baking powder

1 teaspoon baking soda

½ cup unsweetened applesauce

½ cup molasses

⅔ cup low-fat soymilk

3 ounces tofu, sliced and drained between layers of towels

1 tablespoon vegetable oil

1 tablespoon vanilla extract

¼ teaspoon almond extract

2 tablespoons carob chips

Preheat the oven to 350°F. Lightly oil an 8-inch square baking pan or spray with nonstick cooking spray.

In a large bowl, combine the flour, carob powder, baking powder, and baking soda. Mix well.

In a blender, combine the remaining ingredients, except the carob chips. Blend until smooth. Add to the dry mixture, mixing until all the ingredients are moistened. Place in the prepared pan. Sprinkle the carob chips evenly over the brownies. Press them down gently into the brownies. If you want, you may add a few chopped nuts to the batter or to the top of the brownies.

Bake for 30 minutes until a toothpick inserted in the center of the brownies comes out clean. Cool in the pan on a wire rack. Cut into squares to serve.

Per brownie: Calories 104, Protein 2 g,
Fat 2 g, Carbohydrates 21 g

Makes 9 squares

1 cup flour
¼ cup powdered sugar
1 stick margarine, softened

Filling
Egg replacer equal to 2 eggs (see page 135)
½ teaspoon baking powder
1 cup sugar
2 tablespoons fresh lemon juice
1 tablespoon powdered sugar (optional)

Oil an 8- x 8-inch pan. Preheat the oven to 350°F.

Sift the flour and ¼ cup powdered sugar into a 2-quart bowl. Cream in the margarine, using a slotted spoon. When this is well mixed, pat it evenly into the bottom of the baking pan. Set the timer for 20 minutes, and bake this bottom layer. Remove the pan to a board, but don't turn off the oven.

While the crust bakes, mix together the eggs, baking powder, sugar, and lemon juice with a whisk. (This filling will be runny.) Pour the mixture into the baked bottom crust.

Put the pan back in the oven for 20 minutes. (Set the timer.) Remove from the oven, place on a board, and cool for 30 minutes. If desired, sift the 1 tablespoon powdered sugar over the top.

Cut into 9 squares and serve on dessert plates.

Per square: Calories 235, Protein 2 g,
Fat 10 g, Carbohydrates 34 g

137

Cinnamon Buns

Makes 10 buns

Topping
2 tablespoon soy margarine, melted
3 tablespoons maple syrup
2 tablespoons firmly packed brown sugar
2 tablespoons raisins
Ground cinnamon

Filling
1 tablespoon firmly-packed brown sugar
½ teaspoon ground cinnamon
2 tablespoons raisins

Dough
¾ cup whole wheat flour
¾ cup all-purpose flour
1 tablespoon baking powder
1 tablespoon firmly packed brown sugar
3 tablespoons vegetable oil
½ cup orange juice
1 teaspoon vanilla extract

For a real treat, serve these delectable buns piping hot. You won't believe how delicious they are . . . or how easy!

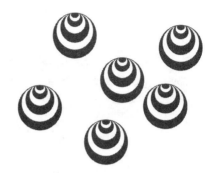

Glaze (optional)
¼ cup confectioners' sugar
1½ teaspoons low-fat soymilk

Have a 9-inch pie pan ready.

To prepare the topping, combine the melted margarine, maple syrup, and brown sugar in a pie pan. Mix well and spread evenly in the pan. Sprinkle evenly with the raisins and cinnamon. Set aside.

To prepare the filling, mix together the brown sugar and cinnamon. Set aside, along with the raisins.

To prepare the dough, combine both types of flour, the baking powder, and brown sugar in a large bowl, mixing well. Add the oil. Mix with a fork or pastry blender until the mixture resembles coarse crumbs. Combine the orange juice and vanilla, and add to the dough. Mix until all the ingredients are moistened. With your hands, work the dough into a ball.

Preheat the oven to 375°F.

Place the dough on a lightly floured surface and knead a few times. Shape the dough into a log. Place a piece of wax paper over the dough and roll into an 8- x 16-inch rectangle. Carefully remove the wax paper. Sprinkle the dough evenly with the filling and raisins.

Starting with one long side, roll the dough up tightly like a jelly roll. Cut the dough into 10 pieces, using a sharp knife and a sawing motion. (This will keep the buns from becoming flattened.) Place the buns, cut side up, evenly in the pan, leaving about ½ inch between buns. With the palm of your hand, press the buns down gently until they are touching each other. Bake for 15 minutes. Let stand 2 to 3 minutes. Then invert onto a serving plate.

To prepare the glaze, place the confectioners sugar in a small bowl or custard cup. Add the milk and mix well. (If a thinner glaze is desired, slowly add more milk, a few drops at a time.)

Drizzle the glaze over the buns, and serve right away. If the buns are to be served later, let them cool before glazing.

Per serving: Calories 163, Protein 2 g,
Fat 6 g, Carbohydrates 24 g

CoFFee CaKe

A very special breakfast treat you can make ahead.

Makes 9 servings

½ cup oil
½ cup sugar
½ cup soymilk
1 cup unbleached flour
1 cup whole wheat pastry flour
2 teaspoons baking powder
½ teaspoon salt
½ cup sugar
½ cup flour
½ teaspoon cinnamon
½ stick margarine, softened

Oil a 9- x 9-inch pan. Preheat the oven to 375°F.

Mix the oil, sugar, and milk with a slotted spoon in a medium bowl. Sift in the 2 cups flour, baking powder, and salt, and stir together. When the batter is well mixed, spread it in the pan.

Mix the sugar, ½ cup flour, cinnamon, and margarine in a small bowl. Sprinkle this mixture evenly over the batter. Set the timer for 45 minutes, and bake in the hot oven. Cut into squares to serve.

Per serving: Calories 347, Protein 4 g,
Fat 17 g, Carbohydrates 43 g

BaNaNa NuT BreaD

For Cranberry Nut Bread, use 1 cup chopped, washed, and drained cranberries instead of bananas.

Makes 1 loaf (16 slices)

½ cup oil

1 cup sugar

1 cup unbleached flour

1 cup whole wheat pastry flour

3 teaspoons baking powder

½ teaspoon salt

2 bananas, well-mashed

½ cup chopped walnuts

Oil a 9- x 5-inch loaf pan. Preheat the oven to 350°F.

In a medium bowl, cream together the oil and sugar using a slotted spoon.

Sift the flour, baking powder, and salt onto a piece of waxed paper. Add the flour mixture to the bowl, and stir until the batter is well mixed and quite smooth. Stir the bananas and walnuts into the batter.

Spoon the mixture into the oiled loaf pan. Set the timer for 45 minutes, and bake in the hot oven. Test for doneness by sticking a toothpick into the center of the loaf. If it comes out clean, the bread is done. Remove the pan from the oven, and let it cool for 10 minutes. Then remove the loaf from the pan.

Per slice: Calories 192, Protein 2 g, Fat 9 g, Carbohydrates 25 g

AppLe CaKe

This makes a delicious breakfast cake, as well as a dessert.

Makes 6 servings

¾ cup sugar

1 cup flour

2 teaspoons baking powder

½ cup water

2 tablespoons oil

1 teaspoon vanilla

2 apples, peeled and cut up

½ cup chopped walnuts

Oil an 8- x 8-inch pan. Preheat the oven to 350°F.

Stir together the sugar, flour, and baking powder. Add the water, oil, and vanilla, and mix well. Add the apples and walnuts to the batter.

Pour into the oiled pan. Set the timer for 35 to 40 minutes, and bake. Cool and cut into squares to serve.

Per serving: Calories 288, Protein 3 g,
Fat 10 g, Carbohydrates 45 g

143

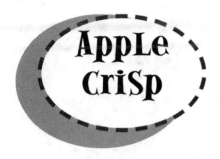

Apple Crisp

The rolled oats you use in this recipe are the same as long-cooking oatmeal (not the instant kind).

Makes 6 servings

6 apples
½ stick margarine
⅓ cup sugar
⅓ cup flour
1 cup rolled oats

Preheat the oven to 350°F.

Oil an 8- x 8-inch pan. Slice the apples into the pan.

Mix the rest of the ingredients in a bowl. Spread this crumbly mixture over the apples.

Set the timer for 40 to 45 minutes, and bake the apples until you can stick a fork through them easily.

Per serving: Calories 265, Protein 3 g, Fat 9 g, Carbohydrates 43 g

FrUit and NuT CanDy BaLLs

Any variety of dried fruit or nut will work in this delicious candy treat. Be creative!

Makes 32 candies

8 large dried figs, cut into quarters (Kitchen shears make this job easy.)

1 cup raisins or chopped apricots, peaches, etc.

1½ cups rolled oats

¼ cup plus 2 tablespoons sliced almonds, walnuts, or soy nuts, etc.

½ teaspoon vanilla extract

⅛ teaspoon almond extract

Combine all the ingredients in a food processor. Using the steel blade, process until the mixture is ground and holds together.

Roll the mixture into 1-inch balls, wetting your hands very slightly as you work to keep it from sticking.

Place the candies on a plate, cover, and store in the refrigerator.

Per serving: Calories 58, Protein 1 g, Fat 1 g, Carbohydrates 9 g

BaNaNa PuDDing

A topping of shredded coconut is the perfect addition to banana pudding.

Makes 4 servings

½ pound tofu, crumbled

2 tablespoons vegetable oil

2 tablespoons orange juice

2 tablespoons maple syrup

2 bananas, sliced

Stir all the ingredients together, then put half in a blender. Turn the blender on and off to blend. When the blender is off, use a rubber scraper to push the mix down the sides. Blend until the mixture is creamy.

Put the pudding into a clean bowl, and blend the rest of the mixture until it is creamy. Then mix the batches together.

Per serving: Calories 184, Protein 5 g, Fat 9 g, Carbohydrates 20 g

SuPer-
QuiCk RiCe
PuDDing

This easy pudding can be made with any leftover grain in place of the rice.

Makes 4 servings

1 (12.3-ounce) package silken tofu

¼ cup confectioners' sugar

2 teaspoons vanilla extract

½ teaspoon ground cinnamon

1½ cups cooked brown rice or other grain

⅓ cup raisins

Blend the tofu until smooth. Spoon into a bowl and add the remaining ingredients. Mix well.

Chill several hours to blend the flavors well.

Per serving: Calories 305, Protein 8 g,
Fat 3 g, Carbohydrates 63 g

HoT CaRob-FuDge SunDae

A rich, delicious, hot, fudgy sauce spooned over soy ice cream or rice milk ice cream makes a truly scrumptious dessert.

Makes 4 servings (2 tablespoons per serving)

3 tablespoons carob powder

1½ teaspoons cornstarch

½ cup low-fat soymilk

3 tablespoons maple syrup

½ teaspoon vanilla extract

1 pint nondairy frozen dessert

In a small saucepan, combine the carob powder and cornstarch, mixing well. Add about 2 tablespoons of the soymilk, and stir until the mixture is very smooth. Gradually add the remaining soymilk, 1 tablespoon at a time, mixing well after each addition. Stir in the maple syrup.

Bring the mixture to a boil over medium-low heat, stirring constantly. Continue to cook, stirring, for 1 minute.

Remove from the heat and stir in the vanilla extract. Spoon the ice cream into serving bowls, and top with the hot sauce.

Per serving: Calories 233, Protein 2 g, Fat 8 g, Carbohydrates 39 g

ToFu WhiPPed TopPing

Silken firm tofu blends easiest and will make this topping incredibly smooth and creamy. Don't hestitate to add other flavors such as ground cinnamon or nutmeg, grated orange peel, or brown sugar.

Makes 1 cup

½ pound tofu, crumbled

3 tablespoons sugar

¼ teaspoon salt

¼ cup vegetable oil

1 teaspoon vanilla

Combine all the ingredients in a blender or food processor, and blend until smooth. Pour into a bowl, and chill.

Per 2 tablespoons: Calories 98, Protein 2 g,
Fat 8 g, Carbohydrates 5 g

LeMon FrosTing

You'll be surprised what a nice contrast this frosting adds to coffee cake, banana bread, or apple cake.

Makes 2 cups

1 teaspoon grated lemon rind

2 cups powdered sugar

2 tablespoons lemon juice

1 tablespoon water

Grate the lemon using the smallest holes of a grater. With a fork, mix it in a small bowl with the powdered sugar, lemon juice, and water.

Per 2 tablespoons: Calories 58, Protein 0 g, Fat 0 g, Carbohydrates 14 g

ChoColaTe FroSting

Here's the perfect topping for your cheesecake. If you like a lighter chocolate flavor, you can experiment with using chocolate-flavored soymilk and omitting the cocoa.

Makes enough to frost a 9- x 13-inch layer cake
or two 8-inch layers

2 tablespoons nonhydrogenated margarine

2 tablespoons soymilk

2 tablespoons cocoa

2 cups powdered sugar

1 teaspoon vanilla

Heat the margarine and soymilk in a medium-size pan. Remove from the heat and beat in the cocoa and powdered sugar a little at a time. When the frosting is creamy, stir in the vanilla.

Drop evenly spaced spoonfuls of the frosting onto the cake, then swirl them together with a spatula.

Per 2 tablespoons: Calories 98, Protein 0 g,
Fat 2 g, Carbohydrates 19 g

151

GETTING EDUCATED

If you are new to a vegetarian diet, there's a lot to learn, and there are many good resources available for novices and experienced vegetarians alike. The organizations listed here are a good starting point and they'll lead you to other good resources.

ORGANIZATIONS YOU SHOULD KNOW

National Center for Nutrition & Dietetics
The American Dietetic Association
216 W. Jackson Blvd., Suite 800
Chicago, Illinois 60606-6995
800-366-1655
Website: www.eatright.org

NCND is the public education arm of the American Dietetic Association. Call for a free copy of the Association's position paper on vegetarian diets and its brochure, *Eating Well—The Vegetarian Way.*

North American Vegetarian Society
P.O. Box 72
Dolgeville, New York 13329
518-568-7970
E-mail: navs@telenet.net

NAVS sponsors the annual Summerfest vegetarian conference, usually held in upstate New York in July. This casual, family-oriented conference draws an international crowd, and nonvegetarians are welcome. It's an excellent opportunity to sample fabulous vegetarian foods and meet other vegetarians. The group also publishes *The Vegetarian Voice,* a newsletter for members.

The Vegetarian Resource Group
P.O. Box 1463
Baltimore, Maryland 21203
410-366-8343
E-mail: vrg@vrg.org
Website: www.vrg.org

VRG is a nonprofit organization that educates the public about vegetarianism and the interrelated issues of health, nutrition, ecology, ethics, and world hunger. The group publishes the bimonthly *Vegetarian Journal* and provides numerous other printed materials for consumers (many printed in Spanish) free of charge or at a modest cost.

Physicians Committee for
    Responsible Medicine
5100 Wisconsin Avenue, N.W.
Suite 404
Washington, D.C. 20016
202-686-2210
Website: www.pcrm.org

PCRM is a nonprofit organization of physicians and others who work together to advocate for compassionate and effective medical practices, research, and health promotion. The group publishes the quarterly newsletter *Good Medicine.*

MAGAZINES AND NEWSLETTERS

Loma Linda University Vegetarian
Nutrition & Health Letter
1711 Nichol Hall
School of Public Health
Loma Linda University
Loma Linda, Calif. 92350
888-558-8703

Vegetarian Nutrition and Health Letter is an 8-page newsletter published ten times per year by the Loma Linda University School of Public Health.

Vegetarian Times
P.O. Box 570
Oak Park, Il. 60303
708-848-8100 or 800-435-9610

Vegetarian Times magazine is a monthly magazine sold on newsstands everywhere.

BOOKS

A Teen's Guide to Going Vegetarian. Judy Krizmanic. Viking, New York, N.Y., 1994.

Becoming Vegetarian. Vesanto Mellina, R.D., Brenda Davis, M. S., R.D., and Victoria Harrison, R.D. Book Publishing Company, Summertown, TN, 1995.

Becoming Vegan. Brenda Davis, R.D., Vesanto Mellina, M.S., R.D. Book Publishing Company, Summertown, TN, 2000

Being Vegetarian for Dummies. Suzanne Havala. Hungry Minds, New York, N.Y. 2001.

Vegan Handbook. Debra Wasserman, M.A., Reed Mangels, Ph.D., R.D. The Vegetarian Resource Group, Baltimore, MD, 1996.

Vegetarian Times Vegetarian Beginner's Guide. Editors of *Vegetarian Times* magazine. Macmillan, New York, N.Y., 1996.

The Vegetarian Way. Virginia Messina, M.PH., R.D. and Mark Messina, Ph.D. Crowne Trade Paperbacks, New York, N.Y., 1996.

FOOD SUPPLIERS

The Mail Order Catalog for
Healthy Eating
P.O. Box 180
Summertown, TN 38483
800-695-2241
www.healthy-eating.com

Call toll-free to request a catalog containing many of the ingredients found in these recipes. Textured soy protein, nutritional yeast flakes, and soymilk are just a few. The catalog also features snacks like vegetarian jerky, soup and pudding cups, instant cereals, and more, as well as a complete selection of vegetarian and vegan cookbooks.

SUZANNE HAVALA, MS, RD, LDN, FADA

A nationally recognized author and consultant on food, nutrition, and public policy, Suzanne has been quoted in *Parade*, *SELF Magazine*, *Shape*, *Vegetarian Times*, *The New York Times*, *Runner's World*, *New Woman*, *YM*, *Omni*, *Sassy*, and *Harper's Bazaar* and in appearances on *Good Morning America*, *Weekend Today in New York*, and the *Susan Powter Show*.

Suzanne has been a vegetarian for over 26 years and is the author of nine books, including *Vegetarian Cooking for Dummies*, *The Natural Kitchen*, and *Shopping for Health: A Nutritionist's Aisle-by-Aisle Guide to Smart, Low-fat Choices at the Supermarket*.

For more information, visit www.suzannehavala.com

DOROTHY R. BATES

Dorothy has written or collaborated on eleven vegetarian cookbooks, including *The TVP Cookbook*, *Tofu Cookery*, *The Tempeh Cookbook*, *The New Farm Vegetarian Cookbook*, and *Kids Can Cook*. She has spent many years teaching young people how to cook their favorite vegetarian dishes in her home in Summertown, Tennessee.

ROBERT OSER

A chef and writer living in Tucson, Arizona, Robert Oser is the author of *Flavors of the Southwest* and *Chili! Mouth-Watering Meatless Recipes*. In addition to owning two health food stores, he has been a demonstration chef at Canyon Ranch Spa and executive chef at the Conspiracy Café, both located in Tucson. Robert is also co-founder of the Vegetarian Resource Group in Tucson and has taught classes in nutrition and vegetarian cooking for over 15 years.

Bobbie Hinman

A pioneer in the field of low-fat cooking, Bobbie is constantly in demand as a speaker and cooking teacher. On a recent media tour for General Mills, she discussed the benefits of eating a low-fat, high-fiber diet. Bobbie is the author of *Burgers 'n Fries 'n Cinnamon Buns*, and is a frequent contributor to *Vegetarian Journal*. She travels extensively, teaching classes and speaking to hospital groups, cardiac centers, weight management centers, colleges, and private organizations.

Our Teen Contributors

Lenny Cramer provided the illustrations for the interior of this book, as well as the inspiration for the cover art. Lenny has been a life-long vegetarian and spends his free time playing lead guitar for his rock group, T.H.B. (The Homegrown Band).

Laura Holzapfel wrote and researched the preface on the impact of a vegetarian diet on animals and the environment. She has also been a vegetarian all her life and is a customer service representative for the Mail Order Catalog, selling vegetarian food products and books.

Laura and Lenny, our teen contributors from the Farm, a vegetarian community in Summertown, Tennessee

INDEX

Purchase these vegetarian cookbooks and nutrition titles from your local bookstore or natural foods store, or you can buy them directly from:

Book Publishing Company
P.O. Box 99
Summertown, TN 38483
1-800-695-2241

Please include $3.50 per book for shipping and handling.

Chili! Mouth-Watering Meatless Recipes
$12.95

Tofu Cookery - $16.95

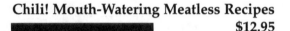

Kids Can Cook - $12.95

Cooking with PETA - $14.95

Becoming Vegetarian
$16.95

Becoming Vegan
$16.95

Burgers 'n Fries 'n Cinnamon Buns
$6.95

To find your favorite vegetarian and soyfood books and products online, visit:

www.healthy-eating.com